Central Cambridge

A Guide to the University and Colleges

by
KEVIN TAYLOR

CAMBRIDGE
UNIVERSITY PRESS

ACKNOWLEDGEMENTS

I am glad to acknowledge the help I have received from Christopher Brooke of Gonville and Caius College, leading historian of the University of Cambridge, and from Liesel Boughton-Fox, Tours Manager at the Cambridge Tourist Information Centre. Bill Davies, Gordon Johnson, Elisabeth Leedham-Green, David McKitterick, Jeremy Mynott, Geoffrey Skelsey, Sarah Taylor, and Tony Wilson read the book in draft and offered good advice, as did representatives of the Cambridge colleges, who kindly checked their own entries. Particularly useful information on individual sites was supplied by Peter Johnson, Roger Lovatt, Robin Matthews, Simon Mitton, Harry Porter, Nicholas Ray, Frank Stubbings, Malcolm Underwood, Robin Walker, and Max Walters.

Martin Walters took the photograph on the front cover, as well as numbers 1, 2, 4, 7, 9, 10, 11, 14, 15, 16, 17, 18, 19, 20, 21, 22, 23, 24, 25, 26, 27, 28, 29, 31, 32, 33, 40, 41, 42, 43, 46, 49, 58, and 61 within the book, and the additional pictures of King's, Corpus Christi, Trinity, the Pitt Building, and Caius which feature on the back cover. Ian Hart took the photographs numbered 30, 36, 38, 45, 47, 48, 50, 51, 52, 53, 54, 55, 56, 57, 59, 62, and 63, and the picture of Jesus College gatehouse on the back. The permission of the Syndics of Cambridge University Library is acknowledged for the illustrations numbered 3, 5, 12, 13, 37, and 44 inside the book, and for the two reproductions inside the back cover. The photograph of the Chancellor in the preliminary pages is reproduced by courtesy of George Shaw; illustration number 6 is from the University of Cambridge Collection of Air Photographs: copyright reserved; number 8 appears by kind permission of the Provost and Fellows of King's College, Cambridge; number 35 by courtesy of Bruce Robertson and the Judge Institute of Management Studies; and number 39 by courtesy of the Sedgwick Museum of Geology.

Marcus Askwith drew the five maps.

Production of the book was in the hands of Lyn Chatterton, Caroline Drake, and Andy Wilson.

I am grateful to all these for their input, as also to the Chancellor, HRH The Prince Philip, Duke of Edinburgh, for supplying a Foreword to the book.

The front cover photograph, by Martin Walters, shows a punt beneath the Bridge of Sighs, St John's College.

The photographs on the back cover are of (top, from left to right): King's College Chapel across the Backs, Corpus Christi College Chapel, and the Wren Library in Trinity College (all by Martin Walters); and (bottom, from left to right): a gargoyle on the Pitt Building, the Gate of Honour in Gonville and Caius College (both by Martin Walters), and the statue of John Alcock on Jesus College gatehouse (by Ian Hart).

CONTENTS

    Map

King's College

Clare College

Trinity Hall

Old Schools

Cockerell Building

Senate-House

Cambridge University Press Bookshop

Great St Mary's (the University Church)

Gonville and Caius College

St Michael's Church

Trinity College

St John's College

Selwyn Divinity School

Round Church (Holy Sepulchre)

Union Society

    Map

St Edward's Church

Arts Theatre

St Bene't's Church

Corpus Christi College

St Catharine's College

St Botolph's Church

Pitt Building

Queens' College

Darwin College

University Centre

Pembroke College

Little St Mary's Church

Peterhouse

Fitzwilliam Museum

Old Addenbrooke's Hospital Site

    Map

Free School Lane and New Museums Site

Whipple Museum of the History of Science

Museum of Zoology

Downing Site

Museum of Archaeology and Anthropology

Sedgwick Museum of Geology

Downing College

Emmanuel College

Christ's College

St Andrew the Great Church

Holy Trinity Church

SANDRINGHAM, NORFOLK

Cambridge is a remarkable mixture of ancient and modern; town and gown; College communities and academic institutions. It is a product of evolution rather than design and there are buildings from every stage of its development since the early middle ages. The University and City give it a unique atmosphere as they continue to adapt to changing circumstances and bring life and meaning to their respective parts of the whole. But it is most certainly not a museum piece nor a tourist trap.

After some 800 years, the University has become a complex organism, and for those who have no experience of its long history or of its contemporary life and activities, a general guide - such as this - is essential to understanding this ancient seat of learning and modern center of research. It describes many of the famous clerics, scholars and builders who have helped to make its architecture and its history, and it also draws a picture of it as a vigorous and energetic part of the educational fabric of our nation and of the international academic community as a whole.

HRH The Prince Philip, Duke of Edinburgh, Chancellor of the University of Cambridge, wearing the Chancellor's robe at a congregation for the conferment of honorary degrees, 13 June 1991.

COLLEGES IN THE UNIVERSITY OF CAMBRIDGE

Name	Location	Date of foundation
Peterhouse	Trumpington Street	1284
Clare College	Trinity Lane	1326
Pembroke College	Trumpington Street	1347
Gonville and Caius College	Trinity Street	1348
Trinity Hall	Trinity Lane	1350
Corpus Christi College	Trumpington Street	1352
King's College	King's Parade	1441
Queens' College	Queens' Lane	1448
St Catharine's College	Trumpington Street	1473
Jesus College	Jesus Lane	1496
Christ's College	St Andrew's Street	1505
St John's College	St John's Street	1511
Magdalene College	Magdalene Street	1542
Trinity College	Trinity Street	1546
Emmanuel College	St Andrew's Street	1584
Sidney Sussex College	Sidney Street	1596
Homerton College	Hills Road	1768
Downing College	Regent Street	1800
Girton College	Huntingdon Road	1869
Newnham College	Sidgwick Avenue	1871
Selwyn College	Grange Road	1882
Hughes Hall	Mortimer Road	1885
St Edmund's College	Mount Pleasant	1896
New Hall	Huntingdon Road	1954
Churchill College	Storey's Way	1960
Darwin College	Silver Street	1964
Lucy Cavendish College	Lady Margaret Road	1965
Wolfson College	Barton Road	1965
Clare Hall	Herschel Road	1966
Fitzwilliam College	Huntingdon Road	1966
Robinson College	Grange Road	1977

Note Dates of foundation given are those normally recognised or celebrated within each college. In reality some colleges were founded in the above dates under different names or on different sites from the ones they now have, while others were re-foundations of earlier institutions on the same site, and others were not formally approved by the University until after their date of foundation. Such details are noted within the individual college entries in this guidebook.

Cambridge is a city of just over 100,000 inhabitants, with a history dating back nearly 2,000 years to Roman times when a small garrison stood on what is now Castle Hill, north west of the Magdalene Bridge crossing of the River Cam. Advantageously placed at the navigable head of a river network leading to the sea, and only 60 miles north of London by road, it grew as a trading post with several churches. Cambridge's position and character, like those of Oxford 80 miles to the south west, were among the factors which drew to it a number of monasteries, as well as groups of scholars and teachers engaged in the pursuit of knowledge, mainly in the fields of theology, church law, civil (i.e. Roman) law, and logic; and by the year 1209 the makings of a University were in place.

Now, almost 800 years later, Cambridge is the home of a University which consists of 31 colleges, where students live, study, and are taught in small groups; of various faculties, departments, and institutes, where particular subjects are researched, lectured on, or taught; and of administrative and ceremonial buildings. The University of Cambridge has a Library, a Press, a Botanic Garden, and eight museums, as well as close connections with four theological colleges, numerous churches, and a major hospital. In total there are about 16,000 full-time students in the University, of whom over 11,000 are undergraduates.

With some notable exceptions, such as the Senate-House, Great St Mary's Church, and the Fitzwilliam Museum, the buildings that attract visitors to Cambridge belong to the colleges. The college system has existed here since the late thirteenth century, and it is this that

---

1 *Senate-House from the south.*

distinguishes Cambridge (as well as Oxford) from other, less ancient universities in which control is more centralised. The relationship between the colleges and other parts of the University is an unusual one. A college is a centre of teaching and learning which also acts as a social and residential unit within the University. Every student is affiliated to a college, and most are provided with food and rooms by their college. However, each of the 31 colleges is self-governing and to a significant extent financially independent, relying not upon central University funding but upon special grants, donations, tuition fees from students, and, in the case of the older colleges, upon bequests, endowments, and investments that have increased in value over many centuries. The colleges are essentially private institutions, while the non-collegiate parts of the University are public, and this interdependent combination of private and public spheres has proved to be one of the strengths of the Cambridge system. A college takes responsibility for the admission and general welfare of its students, offers teaching for them in groups of a manageable size across the whole range of subject areas, and provides a Director of Studies who supervises their academic pursuits. Colleges also provide libraries, to supplement those available elsewhere in the University.

Students from all of the colleges attend lectures or go to laboratories which are not, however, controlled by the colleges, but by the non-collegiate public University via subject-specific units of administration called faculties or departments. Thus, a typical student will matriculate (enrol) in the University of Cambridge as an undergraduate to read (study) a particular subject (such as Natural Sciences, or Engineering, or Classics, or Law) at the age of 18 or 19, having achieved a sufficiently high standard at school level, and that student's life in

Cambridge will then be based in his or her college (e.g. King's, or Emmanuel, or New Hall, or Robinson), but will involve regular attendance at non-collegiate sites determined by the subject he or she is reading (e.g. at the Department of Pathology, or Faculty of Engineering, or Faculty of Classics, or Faculty of Law). A student will complete the degree course by passing the requisite examinations and then graduating in the subject, becoming a graduate. Postgraduates are students who already hold a first degree and who are now studying for some more advanced purpose, such as a doctorate.

There are three terms in the Cambridge academic year: the Michaelmas term, running from October to December; the Lent, from January to March; and the Easter, from April to June. An undergraduate course of study in most cases lasts for three years and involves an examination known as a tripos, which usually results in a degree called the Bachelor of Arts

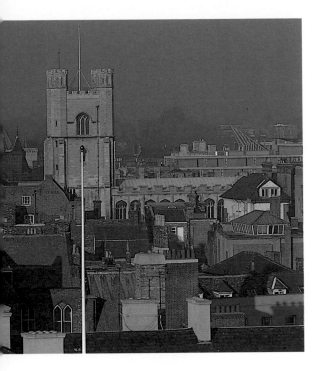

(BA). Tripos examinations take place in about 30 subject areas, and the results help determine whether a student will receive a first-class, second-class, or third-class degree. By far the most populous tripos course is Natural Sciences (accommodating close to 2,000 undergraduates in total), with Medicine, Law, and Engineering usually next in size. Mathematics, Modern and Medieval Languages, History, English, and Economics also attract student numbers in excess of 500. Over 90 per cent of Cambridge undergraduates are from the United Kingdom, the greater part of the annual intake being from British state schools, with a slightly smaller proportion from independent schools. Since the abolition of the Cambridge Entrance Examination in 1985, admission has been determined by performance in school exams such as 'A' Levels, and by interview.

2 *View of central Cambridge from the south, with the towers of St John's College Chapel, Gonville and Caius College Tree Court, and Great St Mary's Church.*

3 *Left to right: Lady Elizabeth de Clare, foundress of Clare College; Bishop William Bateman, founder of Trinity Hall; and Lady Margaret Beaufort, foundress of Christ's and St John's Colleges. Prints from R. Ackerman's* A History of the University of Cambridge *(1815), copied from portraits in the colleges.*

The date of 1209 provides an approximate marker for the origin of the University of Cambridge, for in that year groups of scholars (reputedly migrants from the University of Oxford, which existed slightly earlier) had begun to congregate here for the purpose of study. Teaching in those early days revolved around clerical subjects, and a close relationship between the church and University existed for several hundred years. At least four of

Cambridge's surviving medieval churches served at various times as college chapels.

The college system, modelled on those at Paris and Oxford, began in 1284 with the foundation of Peterhouse, and by 1400 seven of the present-day colleges existed in some form (including Trinity, which did not adopt its modern identity until 1546). The number had risen to 17 by 1800; and in the nineteenth century the University itself underwent a rapid expansion, partly in response to the rise of science in a fast-changing world. In the twentieth century 14 additional colleges were formally affiliated to the University – some of them Victorian institutions newly recognised, others new foundations. The 14 included a teacher-training college (Homerton), a college for mature women (Lucy Cavendish), and five graduate colleges intended mainly for postgraduates (Darwin, St Edmund's, Wolfson, Clare Hall, and Hughes Hall). This brings the total to 31, ranging in size from Trinity, with about 700 undergraduates and 250 postgraduates, to Lucy Cavendish, with about 100 undergraduates and 50 postgraduates.

Only 26 of the colleges have the word 'College' in their familiar title. Four retain the word 'Hall' instead, and then there is Peterhouse. The heads of the colleges also go by different titles, ranging from Master (the most common), to President (six colleges), Principal (two), Mistress (one), Provost (one), and Warden (one).

The picturesque quality of the central colleges is enhanced by their position on the river, which runs from south to north past Darwin, Queens', King's, Clare, Trinity Hall, Trinity, St John's, and Magdalene. These colleges back on to the riverbank, giving rise to the name the Backs, which describes this thousand-metre stretch. Here the river is known as the Cam, but at various times in history it has been called the Granta, a word which now designates a small tributary of the Cam and which is familiar from the name of Grantchester village, a two-and-a-half-mile walk away along delightful meadow paths to the south.

Two of the earliest Cambridge colleges (Michaelhouse, 1324; and King's Hall, 1337) no longer exist, having been amalgamated to form Trinity in 1546. Indeed, the middle of the sixteenth century was a time when all of the colleges were threatened

4 *The Backs: looking south up the river from King's College.*

by an Act of Parliament of 1544 enabling King Henry VIII to dissolve them as he had dissolved the monasteries; but Henry was persuaded to take a progressive view of the collegiate function, turning it to his own ends, and with his foundation of Trinity the colleges became training-grounds for a wider range of professional and courtly roles, bringing the University into its early-modern phase and paving the way for its present-day situation, as a place where both arts and science subjects are studied, taught, and researched to the highest level by students and academics from all over the world.

Although there are now some 70 English universities, Cambridge retains a strong reputation for academic excellence and continues to be placed at or near the top of the government's ratings for quality of teaching and research, receiving one of the highest annual grants from the public purse and remaining, in spite of the special status of its colleges, predominantly a state-funded institution. One of the oldest traditions of scientific research thrives here, in the laboratories of the New Museums Site, Downing Site, and Tennis Court Road, where scientists have worked for over a century, as well as in modern premises such as those on the West Cambridge Site.

The thoroughly co-educational character of the modern University of Cambridge is a relatively recent development. Even though six of the early Cambridge colleges (Clare, Pembroke, Queens', Christ's, St John's, and Sidney Sussex) were founded by women, they remained male institutions for hundreds of years, the colleges only beginning to allow their fellows to marry as late as 1860; and the first women's colleges (Girton and Newnham), although established here in the 1870s, were not fully recognised as part of the University until some 75 years later. In 1881 women were first allowed to sit Cambridge exams, and in 1916, under force of circumstance during the First World War, women were allowed to take medical exams; but they had to wait until 1948 for full admission to degrees and for membership of the University Senate and Regent House (when, to mark the occasion, Queen Elizabeth – now the Queen Mother – was presented with an honorary degree in the Senate-House). In 1960 there were still only three female colleges in the University, the first mixing of the sexes within an undergraduate college occurring in 1972 when Churchill, Clare, and King's admitted women. Change then followed rapidly, and today there remain only three colleges with a single-sex undergraduate composition (Newnham, New Hall, and Lucy Cavendish), all of them for women. Between 40 and 50 per cent of undergraduate students are now female.

Cambridge has one of the most comprehensive systems of academical dress in the world, with distinctive gowns and hoods worn on formal occasions enabling precise identification of a student's degree and in many cases of his or her college. Another tradition is that of May Balls, elaborate night-long entertainments organised by many of the colleges to take place – nowadays always in June – after the summer examinations. Visitors interested in traditional regalia should not miss Ryder & Amies, the University outfitters on King's Parade by Great St Mary's, where the college shields are displayed and where

5 *Academics in their formal dress. Print from R. Ackermann's* A History of the University of Cambridge (1815).

students can buy ties, scarves, and blazers in their college colours. Here also in the window the University sports clubs advertise events and display results.

Important complementary functions of the University are governed by its Press Syndicate, which is responsible for the University's printing and publishing house, Cambridge University Press, an international organisation employing a thousand people; and its Local Examinations and Schools Examinations Syndicates, which produce exams that are sat each year by pupils across the world. The University has a Chancellor, currently Prince Philip, the Duke of Edinburgh, who was installed on 10 June 1977 – his fifty-sixth birthday – and whose predecessors in the role have included Albert, Prince Consort to Queen Victoria. The full-time Vice-Chancellor is the administrative head of the University.

While focusing principally on the central colleges of Cambridge, *Central Cambridge: a*

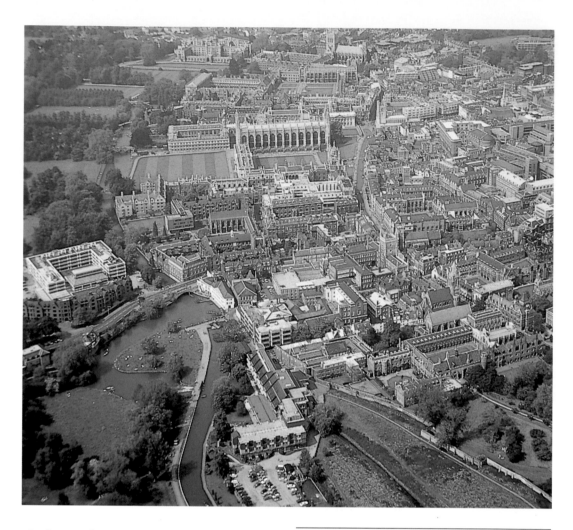

Guide to the University and Colleges also describes many of the important non-collegiate sites to be found here, including libraries, laboratories, and lecture halls. The University's eight museums are described, as is the University collection of air photographs: all are open to the public (though weekend opening is limited). Non-University museums in Cambridge include the Folk Museum on Castle Street below Kettle's Yard and the Museum of Technology on Cheddars Lane (one and a half miles north east along the river).

It is the policy of some colleges to charge visi-

6 *Aerial photograph of Cambridge from the south. The picture shows clearly the north–south orientation of the roads and river, with the Backs colleges following the line of the Cam from Darwin in the south to Magdalene in the north, past King's and St John's.*

tors for entry, or to restrict access in other ways, but this guidebook avoids listing either entry fees or opening hours, since practices change and vary so frequently. It is to be hoped that the visitor, at no matter what time of year, will find enough of the University easily accessible to gain a lasting impression of its historical richness and beauty, along with a sense of its present importance as a place of learning.

KING'S PARADE AND TRINITY STREET

I

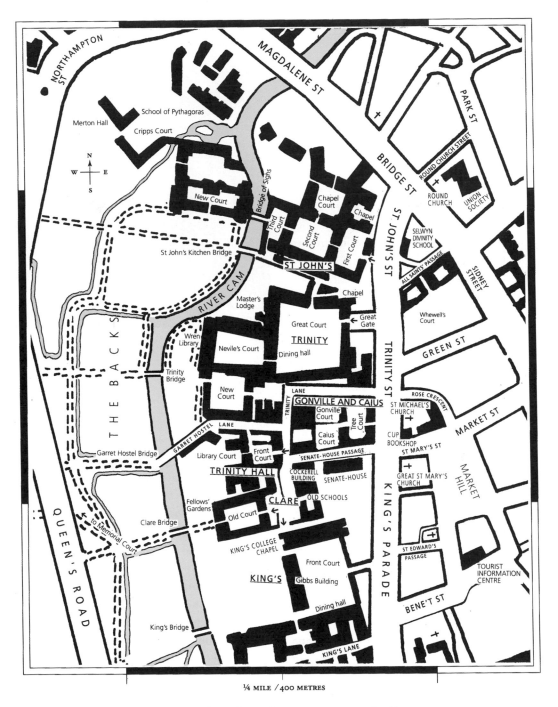

Arrows ➔ indicate the usual tourist entrance to each college.

Both the river and the main streets of Cambridge lie on a north–south axis. The city's main thoroughfare has shifted further eastwards over the years as the University has come to colonise the river banks – until the present day, when the commercial focus of Cambridge for many residents is the Grafton Shopping Centre, almost a mile to the east. In the later Middle Ages, King Henry VI ordained that Milne Street, one of the principal arteries of the medieval city, should be cut off abruptly to make way for a new river site accommodating what would be the biggest and grandest of all the colleges to date, named appropriately: King's College. The interrupted line of Milne Street still runs to the north (now Trinity Lane) and south (Queens' Lane, leading past Queens' College into Silver Street). What was the medieval high street is now King's Parade, running along the east side of the King's site, and from here the visitor may admire the college's elaborate nineteenth-century gothic gate and screen. Though by no means the oldest of Cambridge's 31 colleges, King's remains the focal point for many visitors; it dates from 1441 and is a year younger than Eton College near Windsor, a school (also founded by Henry VI) with which King's has had strong architectural and educational connections.

In the Middle Ages the principal focus of any college was its chapel, and Henry VI himself laid the foundation stone in 1446. King's College Chapel is normally accessible to visitors via the college's north gate, reached by following Senate-House Passage and Trinity Lane. From this gate the building, one of the finest examples of late medieval architecture in the world, looms magnificently ahead. Work began at the east end (nearest King's Parade),

7 West door of King's College Chapel, with Tudor emblems.

so that the building could be consecrated and used for services even as construction continued. Completion took 80 years as the process was constantly interrupted, partly as a result of the diversion of royal funds into warfare. The famous Wars of the Roses raged in England between two families (the Lancasters and the Yorks) claiming succession to the throne. In 1485 the houses combined under a new king, Henry VII, giving rise to the Tudor dynasty, and King's Chapel is emblazoned with the grand heraldic ornamentation of the Tudors. Along the side of the building we see above the windows and doorway elaborate examples of Tudor stone carving: crowns, portcullises, roses, greyhounds, dragons. The differing shades of stone on the walls (white

Yorkshire limestone to the east, darker Northamptonshire limestone further west) bear witness to the separate stages of construction

Inside, soaring shafts create an impression of height and grandeur, and the craftsmanship of fifteenth- and sixteenth-century stone masons is revealed at its best. The carving of the motifs and figures around the walls, the graceful design of the columns, and the intricate fan-vault above our heads (the largest anywhere), all repay close attention. The vault stands 24 metres above the ground, while the chapel extends for 88 metres from end to end, and is 12 metres wide. Above the stone vault (between it and the wooden, lead-capped roof) is a space high enough to walk along. In the windows we see one of the biggest and best collections of sixteenth-century stained glass produced under Flemish inspiration: it depicts, in the upper parts, scenes from the Old Testament and, below them, corresponding New Testament stories. Despite the Biblical subjects, many of the details (costumes, townscapes, a fine Tudor galley) faithfully represent early Renaissance Europe. During the Second World War this priceless glass was taken out and stored piece by piece, although the chapel fortunately avoided damage, as it had in the English Civil War in spite of a visit in 1643 by one of Cromwell's most notorious despoilers, William Dowsing. The fabulous east window above the altar depicts Christ's crucifixion; while the west window (showing the Last Judgement) is an impressive Victorian addition of 1879.

Half way along, the nave is divided from the chancel by a heavy oak screen bearing sets of initials which include (above the passageway)

an intertwined 'H' (for Henry VIII) and 'A' (for Anne Boleyn). The carving can be dated precisely to the mid-1530s, for Henry married Anne in 1533 and had her beheaded in 1536. Other carving on the screen (flowers, beasts, heads of cherubs) is of the finest order, almost certainly the work of continental artists brought from France or Italy by Henry VIII. Surmounting the screen is the huge organ in its seventeenth-century case, frequently used for services, recitals, and concerts, including the famous Festival of Nine Lessons and Carols on Christmas Eve, broadcast live across the world. King's has a choir of international standing, which includes boy singers selected from a special Choir School affiliated to the college.

Passing through the interior of the screen we

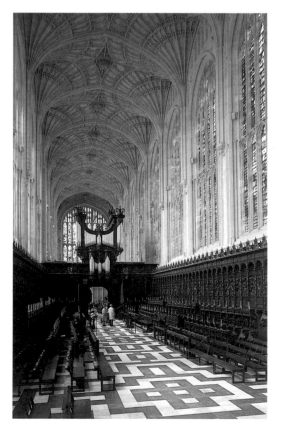

8 *Interior of King's College Chapel, looking west from the high altar.*

find ourselves in the east end, much of it completed before the arrival of the Tudor kings and therefore plainer and sparser in its ornamentation, with the exception of the fine wooden choir stalls, added in the time of Henry VIII (with canopies dating from 1633). Note also the Swedish candles, made of special wax to prevent smoke from blackening the stonework of the chapel. In front of the stalls stands a lectern of the late fifteenth or early sixteenth century, with a small figure of Henry VI on top.

Behind the altar of King's College Chapel stands Rubens's *Adoration of the Magi* (1633–4), left to the college by a wealthy benefactor, having fetched a record price at auction, and placed here (following a debate about its suitability in this setting) in 1968. Finally, it is worth peering into some of the 18 side chapels containing fan-vaulting and precious glass. Through a door to the north of the chancel an exhibition may be visited.

Leaving the chapel and turning to the west, with the great west door (opened for weddings and other ceremonial occasions) behind us, we look across a well-kept lawn to the river, and beyond to rough pasture still grazed by cows, reminding us that nowhere in this East Anglian market town is very far from the country. To the right, the mellow stone of Clare College's Old Court provides a soft contrast with the gothic of King's; and to our left, the stately Gibbs Building of 1724–32 (named after its architect James Gibbs, who also designed the University Senate-House) rises in white Portland stone. Back in Front Court a statue of the founder, Henry VI, perches on top of a fountain, while the Gibbs Building now blocks our view to the river, its elaborately pedimented central arch flanked on each side by ten three-storeyed classical bays creating a

strong impression of width. To the east extend the neo-gothic screens bordering King's Parade, and on the south side stands the dining-hall range. The screens and hall imitate the style of the chapel but were in fact designed more than 350 years after it, by William Wilkins in the 1820s. It is well worth walking round Front Court and along the path to the river at King's Bridge, for a fine view back towards the chapel.

The poet Rupert Brooke, who died in the 1914–18 war, lived in King's until 1909 before moving out to his idyllic Grantchester, the village two and a half miles south of Cambridge immortalised in his poem 'The Old Vicarage, Grantchester'. His acquaintances included E. M. Forster (1879–1970), whose novels The Longest Journey and Maurice draw autobiographically on Cambridge life and who lived in King's into his old age, having first entered the college as a student in 1897.

Despite its grandeur and centrality, King's is no longer one of the largest colleges, and it enjoys a reputation as a relaxed place in which liberal attitudes and a tolerance of informality are combined with high academic standards.

9 *Gibbs Building, King's College, from the west.*

CLARE COLLEGE

Founded in 1326 as University Hall and re-founded in 1338 as Clare Hall, this is the second oldest of Cambridge's 31 colleges. Originally fronting the medieval Milne Street (cut off by the building of King's Chapel), Clare's entrance is now tucked away at the end of Trinity Lane near the north gate of King's. The old buildings were slowly demolished in the seventeenth century, making way for one of the neatest and most satisfying of Cambridge's courtyards, built by local architects Thomas Grumbold and his son Robert between 1638 and 1715. The warmth of the yellow stone is best appreciated from the riverbank on King's College Backs, making the outer south side of the court one of the most photographed buildings in England.

Within, the classicism of Old Court is broken by occasional gothic features, including the fan-vaulting in the gateway – one of the last uses in England of a style brought to perfection in King's Chapel more than 100 years

earlier. While King's had been delayed by the Wars of the Roses, Clare's reconstruction was interrupted by the English Civil War (1642–9), during which Oliver Cromwell plundered the site for building materials to fortify Cambridge Castle. Clare Chapel, reached in the north-east corner of the court, dates from 1763–9 and was designed by James Burrough (the great amateur architect who was Master of Caius College) and built by James Essex. Its tall wooden lantern illuminating the antechapel is a splendid and unusual feature, particularly from inside.

Clare Hall became Clare College in 1856 (and a new Clare Hall was founded separately as a graduate college in 1966). The name comes from Lady Elizabeth de Clare, a wealthy granddaughter of Edward I who endowed the foundation of 1338. All that remains of the medieval court she paid for is a stone panel with a shield representing the college arms, now above the doorway to the small hall, next to the entrance to the main hall accessible via the steps in the middle of the north range. Lady Clare was widowed three times and the periphery of her crest features tears as emblems of mourning.

Clare's most pleasing single feature is its bridge spanning the river, reached through the gateway on the west side of the court, but viewed at its best from King's Bridge to the south or Garret Hostel Bridge to the north – or indeed from a punt on the river. Thomas Grumbold erected this in 1638, and it is now the oldest bridge on the Cam. American novelist Henry James, who had an eye for exquisite structures, admired it and described the way that the line of its balustrade can be seen rising and then 'gently collapsing' in the central section.

It is worth following Clare Avenue (laid out in 1690) through the iron gates (erected in 1714),

past the beautiful Fellows' Gardens, and on across Queen's Road to the site of Clare Memorial and Thirkill Courts (1923–55), built to release the college finally from its long-standing confinement within the solitary Old Court. The architect who inaugurated this scheme was Giles Gilbert Scott, shortly afterwards responsible for the new University Library just to the west. Clare now grew rapidly, the new building work of the 1950s funded largely by American philanthropist Paul Mellon, a member of the college. This site helped to accommodate women undergraduates when Clare opened its doors to them in the autumn of 1972 – the first undergraduate college, along with King's and Churchill, to become co-residential. Memorial Court (to the north) has now been divided into two parts, re-designated Memorial Court and Ashby Court, by the addition of a library block in 1986. One effect has been to diminish the visual dominance of the University Library

10 *Clare Bridge from the north.*

over the site. The statue on the Queen's Road side is Henry Moore's *The Falling Warrior.*

Like many of the ancient colleges in central Cambridge, Clare has another site lying away from the centre. This is known as The Colony and is situated near the corner of Castle Street and Chesterton Lane behind St Giles's Church, on land that has been in Clare's ownership for hundreds of years and which now houses more than half of the college's undergraduates.

Clare's former members include Hugh Latimer, the Protestant reformer burned at the stake by Mary I in 1555, and Nicholas Ferrar, founder in 1625 of the Anglican community at Little Gidding (subject of one of T. S. Eliot's poems in *Four Quartets*). Ferrar was a fervent supporter of colonial expansion in Virginia, and

Clare retained strong connections with the New World, offering places throughout the eighteenth century to the sons of eminent American families.

Clare holds the record for the longest-serving Master: Dr Edward Atkinson occupied the Master's lodge here for an extraordinary 59 years from 1856 to 1915.

TRINITY HALL

Traditionally a college strong in the study of Law, Trinity Hall lies due north of Clare. It is quite distinct from Trinity College, which it pre-dates by some 200 years, but whose existence prevented it from following the nine-teenth-century trend of changing its name from 'Hall' to 'College'. This is the only ancient Cambridge college still to be known as a Hall.

William Bateman, Bishop of Norwich, who was to oversee the early years of neighbouring Gonville Hall after the death of Edmund Gonville, decided in 1350 to found his own college devoted to Law. Although this empha-sis changed in the mid-nineteenth century, Trinity Hall retains a reputation for legal studies, producing a fine array of judges, barristers, and lawyers. Among its most famous products (and certainly the most powerful) was Stephen Gardiner (1497–1555), who was Master of Trinity Hall as well as Chancellor of the University, Bishop of Winchester, Lord Chancellor of England, chief advisor to Henry VIII and Mary I, and said by some to be the English Machiavelli. A later fellow of the col-lege was Leslie Stephen, editor of the *Dictionary of National Biography*, whose daugh-ter Virginia met her future husband Leonard Woolf in Cambridge. Virginia Woolf evokes the city and University in her *Jacob's Room*

(1922) and *A Room of One's Own* (1929), the latter of which was derived from lectures she delivered in Cambridge.

At the bend in Trinity Lane where Trinity Hall joins Clare, the visitor will notice collars of metal spikes around the drainpipe running past the first-floor rooms: a measure to prevent students climbing into their lodgings late at night after the porter's lodge has closed. 'Night-climbing' is a favourite (if illicit) pur-suit among students, who have been known to scale the heights of King's College Chapel to suspend items – including a line of washing and a 'Ban the Bomb' banner – between the pinnacles. Once an Austin 7 car was hauled by night onto the roof of the Senate-House.

Trinity Hall's Front Court (beyond the porter's lodge) dates from the period after the founda-tion of 1350 but was ashlar-faced and otherwise converted in more recent times, visible evi-dence of the fourteenth century being limited to an exposed gothic window on the first floor in the north-west corner, sunk behind the later additions, and (through a passage in the north wall) the outer face of the range, on which the original clunch (hard chalk) fabric is almost totally revealed. These elements show the lay-ered effect typical of many college buildings in Cambridge, with alterations and restorations compounding earlier work.

A quiet chapel, probably begun in 1352 (making it the earliest of the college chapels – it is also one of the smallest) is entered in the south-west corner of Front Court. In the antechapel two windows commemorate the elevation of Robert Runcie, formerly Dean of Trinity Hall, to the Archbishopric of Canterbury (1980). The college crest displayed prominently on the painted roof of the chapel and on the pediments and wall of the court features a gorget (a crescent-shaped piece of armour worn around the throat), often coupled with Bishop Bateman's mitres. On the north side of the court the crest appears above a numbered plaque: this is the college's insurance number, identifying it in case of fire and dating from the days when the fire brigades were controlled by insurance companies with their own symbols – in this case a sun.

An archway beneath the western pediment leads to Library Court featuring, on the right-hand side, the architectural highlight of the college, its library (*c.*1600) in Elizabethan red brick with a stepped gable at the far end. Further on, seats overlook the river at Garret Hostel Bridge, while the Fellows' Garden lies over the wall to the south. Author Henry James wrote in 1883 that 'If I were called upon to mention the prettiest corner of the world, I should draw a thoughtful sigh and point the way to the garden of Trinity Hall.' Unlike most other Backs colleges, Trinity Hall stops here and does not own land on the west side of the river.

Expansion at Trinity Hall is limited by its position, but the small site has been skilfully developed, with unobtrusive modern extensions along the Garret Hostel Lane edge. In 1948 a larger site between Huntingdon Road and Storey's Way, Wychfield, was purchased by the college.

OLD SCHOOLS

On Trinity Lane, almost opposite the entrance to Clare, stands a gateway leading to the administrative core of the University of Cambridge: the Old Schools. This site is also the historical centre of the University, for it incorporates buildings begun in about 1350 and in use as lecture rooms by 1400, representing

11 *The Library, Trinity Hall.*

12 *The end of Trinity Lane, showing the medieval gatehouse (now part of the Old Schools) before Scott's renovation and extension, with King's College Chapel beyond. Print of 1825 from R. B. Harraden's* Illustrations of the University of Cambridge *(1830).*

13 *Looking across Senate-House Passage from Caius Court, Gonville and Caius College, with the Gate of Honour in the foreground. The medieval Old Schools clearly visible to the right of the Senate-House are today virtually obscured by the Cockerell Building of 1837–42. Print of 1810 from R. B. Harraden's* Cantabrigia Depicta: A Series of Engravings *(1809–11).*

the earliest surviving attempt to provide a central forum where students and scholars from all of the colleges, halls, and hostels that were springing up around Cambridge could come together for a common education. The gatehouse dates from 1441 and was until 1829 part of King's College, but it remained incomplete for 400 years, the lower half being restored and the upper half built anew (1864–7) by George Gilbert Scott. The Old Schools site is the first

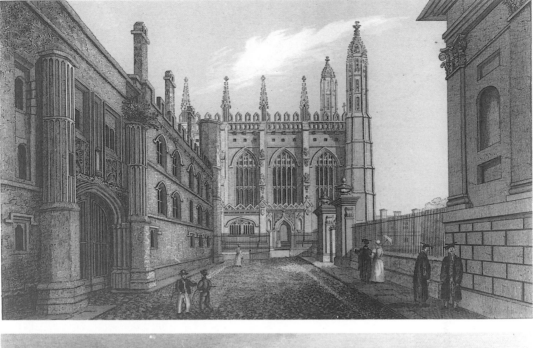

of many in Cambridge which belong not to any particular college but to the public University itself.

Half way up nearby Senate-House Passage, a gap with steps affords a view of the arcaded eighteenth-century façade of the Old Schools (1754–8), behind which can just be seen a portion of the old rubble wall of the lecture rooms completed by 1400, including a gothic

window. This, the range containing the original Divinity School, is the oldest building to survive from the early public University (though some of the colleges feature earlier work). The various buildings around the Old Schools yards nowadays house offices and formal rooms, including the University Combination Room on the first floor of the Divinity School, the University Registry, and the Council Room: these are not open to visitors.

COCKERELL BUILDING

The word BIBLIOTHECA (Latin for library) is inscribed appropriately above the doorway of the large structure which flanks the south-western side of Senate-House Passage and towers in the foreground above the Old Schools. This is the Cockerell Building (1837–42), the work of Victorian architect C. R. Cockerell, constructed to house the rapidly

14 *Students seeking out their tripos results, posted on boards along the south wall of the Senate-House.*

expanding University Library which had previously been contained within the neighbouring Old Schools precincts since 1438. The main University book collections moved to their present site in west Cambridge in the 1930s and the roomy Cockerell Building was subsequently host to the library of the History Faculty until it moved to the Sidgwick Site in the 1960s; to that of the Law Faculty until the mid-1990s; and thereafter to the library of adjacent Gonville and Caius College, which purchased a 350-year lease on the building from the University in 1992.

SENATE-HOUSE

The Senate-House is the ceremonial centre of Cambridge, where degrees are conferred on students and distinguished visitors, where formal votes are taken on decisions affecting the life of the University, and where important public lectures are delivered. Here undergraduates first discover their examination results, listed on special boards placed along the south wall, at the end of the academic year in May and June; here too students from each college process in their academic gowns to receive a certificate of graduation from the University of Cambridge, in a special ceremony during which the Vice-Chancellor of the University or his deputy makes an official pronouncement in Latin.

The 'Senate' is the collective name given to all holders of Cambridge degrees at MA level or higher. The Senate is represented for practical purposes by the 'Regent House', whose membership is invited to the Senate-House building when contentious issues relating to the legislation, constitution, and actions of the University need to be voted upon. Thus, the Senate-House is, both symbolically and actually, the very hub of the University of Cambridge, where important administrative and academic policies are determined and decisions taken with appropriate formal aplomb.

The building itself is, in some ways even more than King's Chapel, the architectural centrepiece of Cambridge. Built between 1722 and 1730 in a restrained baroque style by James Gibbs, with the help of James Burrough, its well-proportioned windows, pediments, parapet, and Corinthinan pilasters and columns present a stately effect rising from the neat lawn with its central urn and its black railings of 1730 (among the first to be put up in England). Inside, an ante-room leads into a spacious hall with galleries on either side.

The Senate-House had been intended by Gibbs as part of a three-sided court of buildings, but this, like Cockerell's later scheme to cover the site of the Old Schools with Victorian structures, and Nicholas Hawksmoor's earlier one to convert the centre of Cambridge into a grand classical forum, never came about. Additions subsequent to the Senate-House were limited to Stephen Wright's east-facing façade of the Old Schools and Cockerell's University Library. The view across the whole site from King's Parade, with the railings and lawn in the foreground, is the most stately in Cambridge. The Senate-House stands to the north, while Wright's well-matched Old Schools façade forms a western border, the high windows, cornice, and parapet of its upper section rising above a five-arched open undercroft. Meanwhile the gothic grandeur of King's College Chapel looms behind a massive horse-chestnut tree on its lawn to the south.

CAMBRIDGE UNIVERSITY PRESS BOOKSHOP

On the corner opposite the Senate-House lies the oldest bookshop site in England, where books have been sold since at least 1581. Former occupants have included the Macmillan brothers, Alexander and Daniel, who set up here in 1845 before moving to London to make their fortune as publishers. Since 1992 the building has been the bookshop of the oldest printer and publisher in the world, the University's own press, Cambridge University Press, which received its royal charter from Henry VIII in 1534 and began printing books on a site near here (where the Senate-House lawn now lies) in 1584. The University Press has one of the largest outputs of any international publisher, and here the entire range of its list of some 12,500 publications in print is stocked. This

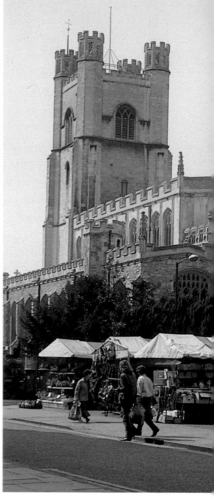

bookshop, along with the Pitt Building on Trumpington Street, represents the Press in central Cambridge; but the publishing and printing divisions are now based a mile and a half to the south on Shaftesbury Road, while branches in North America and Australia and many offices and representatives in other parts of the world continue to expand the operation abroad. The Press's publications have included the Geneva Bible (1591), Milton's *Lycidas* (1638), the *Book of Common Prayer* (1638), Newton's *Principia Mathematica* (second edition, 1713), G. E. Moore's *Principia Ethica* (1903), and the New English Bible (1961–70). There is an exhibition of the Press's history on the first floor, including a map of its international operations.

GREAT ST MARY'S (THE UNIVERSITY CHURCH)

Although overshadowed in grandeur by King's College Chapel across the road, the Church of St Mary the Great is an important late gothic building begun in 1478 and lying at the very heart of Cambridge. An earlier church had existed on the same site since at least 1205 and probably much earlier, and it is likely that the medieval Old Schools were deliberately placed in the vicinity of this focal point. Certainly by 1478 the scholars were

15 (top left) *The east front of the Senate-House, with the Cambridge University Press Bookshop in the foreground.*

16 (above) *Great St Mary's Church, with the market place in the foreground.*

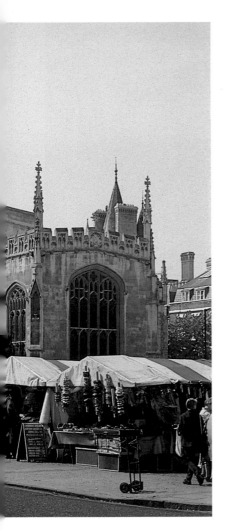

ready to build here a special 'University Church'; and until the Senate-House was built 250 years later, University degree ceremonies were held inside Great St Mary's. Sermons are still preached to the University by visiting speakers on Sunday evenings during term from the pulpit, which can be moved along on rails; and although it is an Anglican parish church, Great St Mary's receives a special financial contribution towards its regular running and maintenance costs from the University.

The top of the church tower (reached by 123 spiral steps) offers the best of all views of the surrounding colleges. From this tower were first heard the 'Westminster' chimes familiar today as those rung by Big Ben in London, and also now heard from Sydney and Adelaide town halls in Australia, rung in the bell-towers of various American universities, and frequently broadcast before the time-signal on British radio programmes – they were designed for Great St Mary's by Dr Joseph Jowett of Trinity Hall in 1793. A curfew calling students back to their colleges was rung from the tower at nine in the evening for several hundred years, until 1939.

The church's high aisle arches and spacious clerestory windows are light and elegant, offset by the dark timber of the roof (donated in 1505 by Henry VII in the form of 100 oaks) and pews. Tiered galleries in the aisles date from the eighteenth century, when the seating capacity was increased to 1,700, and in this period the building was considered roomy enough to house a fire engine at one end. While King's College Chapel marks an important national development in architectural history, St Mary the Great belongs to the great East Anglian tradition of church building of the late fifteenth century, and can be viewed in the context of other regional masterpieces on a similar scale, such as the churches at Lavenham and Saffron Walden. A typically East Anglian feature is the poppy-head carving at the ends of some of the pews.

Outside, a circular mark on the south-west buttress of the tower is the official centre-point of Cambridge from which distances were first measured in 1725 by a series of milestones, said to be the first in Britain since Roman times. Many of them still exist along the roads towards London, Huntingdon, and Essex.

GONVILLE AND CAIUS COLLEGE

Gonville and Caius (usually abbreviated to Caius, pronounced 'Keys') is the fourth oldest of the colleges. The only college in Cambridge or Oxford to include the names of two founders in its title, it occupies a central position, both geographically and, with a student population of some 650 and significant wealth, in the life of the University.

Founded in 1348 (the year in which the Black Death broke out in England) by a Norfolk priest called Edmund Gonville, the original Gonville Hall provided premises in Cambridge for trainee priests supported largely by money raised from tenants on church estates in rural Norfolk – money which was to sustain the college for the next 200 years. Gonville's aim was to send men educated here back into the locality to serve as clergy and scholars. He died in 1351 and work on his college was continued by Bishop William Bateman, who had founded neighbouring Trinity Hall in 1350.

The 1390s saw the completion of the chapel, reached via Tree Court (with its lovely avenue of whitebeams unusual among Cambridge's normally treeless inner yards) and Caius Court. Inside the chapel visitors may pull back a hinged wooden panel beneath the kneeling tomb-figure of benefactor Thomas Legge on the right-hand side to reveal a section of the late fourteenth-century wall still standing beneath more recent embellishments. Also of note in the chapel are the splendid alabaster tomb of the second founder, John Caius, with its classical columns and surmounting skull; the golden cherubs of 1637 adorning the ceiling; and the imposing organ installed in 1981.

A right turn outside the chapel leads to

17 *Statue of John Caius holding a model of the Gate of Honour, Gonville and Caius College, near the infamous Senate-House Leap.*

Gonville Court, the core of the original college of 1348, faced with ashlar in the eighteenth century and now splendidly adorned with window boxes and planted borders.

Gonville Hall was enlarged and transformed by John Keys, an eminent physician who had studied in Italy, immersing himself in the humanist learning of the Renaissance and Latinising his name to Caius. The new College of Gonville and Caius, endowed with Dr Caius's money, received its charter from Mary I in 1557. Caius brought a new spirit to Cambridge, rejecting the medievalism of castellated gatehouses and enclosed courtyards (as at Queens' and St John's) and commissioning the construction of a three-sided court, Caius Court, on the Italian model (the fourth side left open to allow air to circulate) and of three stone gates in an eclectic classical style representing Humility, Virtue, and Honour, with Latin inscriptions of these attributes above each gate. This scheme led the student both symbolically and literally from a Humble entrance ('Humilitas' – where the porter's lodge now stands on Trinity Street), to a Virtuous daily passage within the college ('Virtutis' – between Tree and Caius Courts), and finally to an Honourable procession under the triumphal arch ('Honoris' – on the formerly open south side of Caius Court, now flanked by a wall) when he graduated. On the Gate of Virtue may be seen the date of construction, 1567; and through the Gate of Honour (depicted on p.17) graduating Caians still process each summer on their way to collect their degrees from the adjacent Senate-House.

Other notable 'Caians' have included William Harvey, who discovered the circulation of the blood; Titus Oates, who hatched the infamous Popish Plot alleging a Catholic conspiracy to kill King Charles II; Edward Wilson, doctor to Captain Scott's ill-fated Antarctic expedition, who flew the college flag at the South Pole in 1912 and died nearby; James Chadwick, the nuclear physicist who discovered the neutron; Joseph Needham, the great historian of Chinese science and civilisation; and Stephen Hawking, physicist and best-selling author of *A Brief History of Time*.

Leaving the college and standing on the cobbles at the head of Senate-House Passage, beneath the black-turreted Victorian tower with its statues of Caius, Gonville (below), and Bishop Bateman, we may look up at the infamous 'Senate-House Leap', a gap of some two and a half metres between a small turret window and the ledge of the Senate-House roof. A custom – now strictly outlawed owing to the number of casualties – once dared Caius undergraduates to jump across this gap and (more difficult) back again.

Although the first college to abolish celibacy among its fellows (in 1860), Caius was slow to admit women, who first came here as undergraduates only in 1979. Recent expansion includes a lease on the Cockerell Building on Senate-House Passage, to house the college library.

ST MICHAEL'S CHURCH

St Michael's, on the east side of Trinity Street, once doubled as a college chapel and a parish church. It served two colleges: Michaelhouse, a foundation of 1324 absorbed into Trinity College in 1546; and Gonville and Caius, in its early incarnation as Gonville Hall. The architecture (1324–50) is of the decorated gothic period, with characteristic reticulated tracery in the windows. The building is now used by the parish of Great St Mary's, with services held in the eastern Hervey de Stanton Chapel, named after the founder of Michaelhouse. Behind the church stands St Michael's Court (1903), belonging to Gonville and Caius.

TRINITY COLLEGE

A tour of the largest and wealthiest of the colleges, Trinity, is best begun on the cobbles outside the Great Gate on Trinity Street. Generations of renowned thinkers have passed through this gatehouse, for Trinity College's list of alumni reads like a *Who's Who* of British intellectual and literary history. Members of Trinity have included Francis Bacon and Isaac Newton; the philosophers G. E. Moore,

18 (left) *Great Gate, Trinity College, with statue of Henry VIII and arms of Edward III.*

19 (top) *Great Court, Trinity College.*

Bertrand Russell, and Ludwig Wittgenstein; historians Thomas Babington Macaulay and his great-nephew George Macaulay Trevelyan; anthropologist J. G. Frazer; poets George Herbert, Andrew Marvell, John Dryden, Lord Byron, Alfred Tennyson, A. E. Housman, and Thom Gunn; and writers William Thackeray, A. A. Milne, and Vladimir Nabokov. The best-known undergraduate in modern times was Prince Charles, who came up in 1967 and graduated with a degree in History and Archaeology in 1970; his grandfather King George VI and great-great grandfather Edward VII also studied here. Indian Prime Ministers J. Nehru and Rajiv Gandhi were Trinity under-graduates. Trinity College has produced 28 Nobel Prize winners, beginning in the early twentieth century with the outstanding

physicists Lord Rayleigh (1904), J. J. Thomson (1906), Ernest Rutherford (1908), and William Bragg (1915). In the 1820s and 30s Trinity helped spawn the Cambridge Apostles, a discussion group which was to play a part in forming the minds of many leading members of the British intelligentsia, including – in our own century – the infamous spies Guy Burgess and Anthony Blunt.

Trinity was founded in 1546 by King Henry VIII, whose statue stands over the Great Gate. The king holds in his left hand a golden orb surmounted by a cross representing universal Christianity, and in his right a royal sceptre; but the latter symbol has been replaced by something more mundane: a chair leg standing in for the original which student pranksters have removed. Beneath Henry we see the royal coat-of-arms representing Edward III, founder of an earlier college on this site, King's Hall.

Edward, king of England during the Black Death and Hundred Years' War, also laid claim to France, and was the first English king to quarter the rampant lions with the French fleur-de-lys, producing the now-familiar arms. Aligned beneath are the shields of his six sons, including the Black Prince (the first Prince of Wales, whose white feathers and motto are still used by Prince Charles today) and a blank white shield (a symbolic heraldic device showing that the bearer – here the young Earl of Hatfield – died in infancy).

The Great Gate was begun in 1518 at the entrance to King's Hall, its size and fortified grandeur – of a kind normally reserved for castles or important manor houses – bearing witness to the esteem in which the Cambridge colleges were held in the later Middle Ages. Henry VIII incorporated King's Hall, along with another old college on the site,

Michaelhouse, into the new Trinity in 1546. On the grass near the gate stands an apple tree planted in 1954 and descended from one in the garden of Isaac Newton's home, Woolsthorpe Manor in Lincolnshire. It commemorates the falling apple which is said to have inspired Newton's theory of gravity. The great scientist lived in rooms just north of the Great Gate between 1679 and 1696, and worked here on his *Principia Mathematica*.

Passing through the gate, we enter the largest enclosed courtyard in Europe. Trinity Great Court, with a circumference of 370 metres, is the site of a foot race celebrated in the film *Chariots of Fire*. Here athletes attempt to run round the perimeter path before the clock on the tower beside the chapel has struck 24 times, which it does at midday and midnight, taking 45 seconds. The race was staged in 1988 between two top runners, Sebastian Coe and Steve Cram, who barely managed to achieve the feat first recorded by Olympic hurdler Lord Burghley back in 1927.

The court contains all the features typical of Cambridge college architecture. On either side of the Great Gate (with its west-facing statues of James I with his wife Anne of Denmark and son Charles) run ranges of rooms occupied by students and fellows. To the north the chapel, begun in 1555 during the reign of Queen Mary I, presents its gothic windows and pinnacles: inside, the visitor may seek out statues of Bacon, Newton (by Roubiliac), Macaulay, and Tennyson, and gaze from the antechapel into the interior with its splendid roof, stalls, and reredos. Next to the chapel stands another gatehouse, the earliest in Cambridge, built originally between 1427 and 1437 for King's Hall; and on the west range lies the creeper-clad Master's lodge. Trinity's Master is not elected by the fellows but appointed by the Crown. As a political appointment, the Mastership of Trinity might fall to a retiring public figure, as in the case of R. A. Butler, a former Chancellor of the Exchequer, who occupied this lodge in the 1960s. A new Master arriving at Trinity must knock ceremoniously on the doors of the Great Gate before gaining admittance.

The court has an elegant central fountain (1601–15; rebuilt 1715), whose water comes from an underground conduit one and a half miles long, first constructed in the fourteenth century by

20 *Wren Library seen across Nevile's Court, Trinity College.*

Franciscan friars to serve their monastery where Sidney Sussex College now stands; and yet another gatehouse on the south range, featuring a statue of Queen Elizabeth I, daughter of the founder. South of the Master's lodge stands the Elizabethan dining hall (1604–5), with interior minstrels' gallery and hammer-beam roof. The glass lantern on top is a particularly attractive feature. A passage, flanked by an oak screen rich in strap-panelling, divides the hall and kitchens. The dessert dish 'crème brûlée' is, despite its French name, said to have been invented in these kitchens.

Beyond the hall to the west lies Nevile's Court,

named after Dr Thomas Nevile, Master of Trinity from 1593 to 1615, who sponsored a massive programme of building and expansion. This court has the air of a spacious Roman bathhouse with its high colonnades and classical façades. Here the poet Lord Byron lived, in a suite of rooms on the first floor of the north side, during his time at Trinity (1805–7).

Originally three-sided, Nevile's Court was prolonged and closed at its west end in 1676–95 by the Wren Library, named after its designer, the great architect Christopher Wren. It is his finest architectural achievement outside London. Classical figures, representing (from left to right) Divinity, Law, Physic (i.e. Medicine), and Mathematics, surmount the library, which rests at first-floor level on a row of Tuscan columns in front of grilled openings with views through to the river. The library interior offers an immediate sense of spaciousness, since the floor is sunk deeper and the windows raised higher than has appeared from outside – a trick of perspective by this technically most ingenious of architects. Wren designed the bookcases, which feature superb wood carving by Grinling Gibbons. A number of marble busts sit at the ends of the book-case cubicles, including one of Newton by Roubiliac (1751). The life-size statue of Byron (1831) by Danish sculptor Bertil Thorwaldsen should also be noted.

On the east side of Nevile's Court, we see Wren's Tribune, the classical platform and staircase built against the west side of the dining hall; and through the southern arches New Court, designed in 1821 by William Wilkins. New Court's western gatehouse leads to the Backs, where excellent views of the library (the peach-coloured hues of its Ketton stone catching the light) and of the lawns stretching north towards St John's can be obtained from Trinity Bridge.

A tour of Trinity is best concluded back near the Great Gate on Trinity Street, where the range opposite is Whewell's Court, named after William Whewell, Master from 1841 to 1866, who helped introduce the study of Natural Sciences at Cambridge. With 700 undergraduate students, over 250 post-graduates, and extensive holdings of property in Cambridge and elsewhere, Trinity remains the largest of the colleges and uses its considerable resources to provide numerous scholarships and grants in the service of higher education.

ST JOHN'S COLLEGE

St John's is entered from St John's Street through the most colourful of Cambridge gate-houses, its orange bricks framing the carved heraldic arms of Lady Margaret Beaufort (mother of Henry VII), the college's foundress. It is worth pausing on the opposite side of the street to examine the carving, painted to reflect as accurately as possible the original colour-scheme, which features two mythological beasts with surreally horned heads, antelopes' bodies, and the tails of elephants or lions, supporting the royal crest and crown, and flanked by the distinctive portcullises of the Tudor dynasty descended from Lady Margaret. These strange conglomerate animals known as 'yales' are also the symbol of the northern lord-ship of Kendal, which was one of Margaret's many estates: they stand in a field of coloured flowers which include marguerite daisies, a pun on the name of the foundress. The gatehouse was built at the foundation of the college in 1511. Margaret's legacy to Cambridge also included Christ's College, whose gatehouse sports an almost identical coat-of-arms. A devout woman, she promoted the study of divinity: her confessor was John Fisher, Bishop of Rochester and one of her executors, who supervised the foundation of St John's after her death in 1509. The college competes in rowing events under the name 'The Lady Margaret Boat Club' rather than St John's, owing to an incident in which the St John's crew was banned from the river.

On this site in the Middle Ages stood a hospi-tal named after St John the Evangelist, who was adopted as the new college's patron. A stat-ue of him holding a poisoned chalice (with the head of a serpent – into which St John is said to have converted the poison – emerging over the rim) stands in the canopied niche above

the Tudor arms. His and the college's symbol, an eagle, stands near his feet.

Through the gate we enter First Court, once a four-sided yard closed to the north by the old hospital and college chapel, whose foundations are still marked on the lawn. Older buildings remain on three sides, but the fourth was opened up in the 1860s to make room for a massive new chapel in monumental Victorian gothic by the celebrated architect George Gilbert Scott. The pinnacled tower dominates not only this corner of the college, but the whole of the north end of the city centre, and is a prominent landmark from afar. Lifelike statues of notable former members of St John's ('Johnians') stand in niches around the outer wall. A dining hall with two bay windows adjoins the chapel, the window nearest the chapel porch being a Victorian addition replicating the Tudor one further south. In medieval manor houses the bay window was aligned with the High Table to illuminate the dais where the nobles sat, and here the southerly window marks the end of the original hall while the northerly one lets light on to the present High Table at the end of the nineteenth-century extension. Students eating here in the early years could be confined to a diet of bread and water as a punishment for petty offences within the college, which included speaking English rather than one of the classical languages they were studying, or wearing their hair too long. More serious crimes listed in the original college statutes include 'Theft, murder, incest, notorious adultery or fornication, scaling the walls or opening the gate at night ... to be punished with expulsion'!

21 *St John the Evangelist on the gatehouse of St John's College.*

An archway beneath a figure of Lady Margaret Beaufort separates the hall from the kitchens, and high up in the south-western corner of First Court on what is now 'F' staircase the poet William Wordsworth discovered his 'nook obscure' when he came to live in St John's as a student in 1787:

> Right underneath, the College kitchens made
> A humming sound, less tuneable than bees,
> But hardly less industrious.
>   (*The Prelude*, Book III)

Another famous W.W., the anti-slavery campaigner William Wilberforce, was a near-contemporary of Wordsworth's at St John's.

Inside the chapel, the dark woodwork, deeply coloured glass, and eastern apse have a heavy grandeur characteristic of mid-nineteenth-century church building. Here the chapel choir – second only to that of King's in world renown – sings, its treble boy choristers drawn from St John's College School, an establishment across the river founded for this purpose. The north-western chapel exit leads through Chapel Court, with a library extension of the mid-1990s matching the nearby red-brick range of Second Court, 400 years its senior.

Now we enter Second Court, where on the north side a bay window fronts the first-floor Long Gallery, a room in which the marriage contract between King Charles I of England and Henrietta Maria of Spain is said to have been signed, and in which some of the D-Day landings during the Second World War were planned. Another gatehouse (1598–1602), with a statue of the Countess of Shrewsbury who paid in part for Second Court's construction but failed to meet the full amount of £3,400 she had promised, looms above the passage into the smaller Third Court (1669–72). Built

22 *St John's College Chapel, by George Gilbert Scott.*

over a period of 150 years and maintaining the use of red brick and cobbles, the three-court scheme gave St John's a sense of architectural unity lacking in other colleges, and also provided plentiful living space for students. St John's has long vied with Trinity for the title of 'largest college', and with over 800 students is the second largest in the University by some margin – though still more than 100 short of Trinity.

A left turn across the cobbles of Third Court takes us round a corner and on to the early eighteenth-century Kitchen Bridge, from which a new vista opens across the lawns and down-river to the much-photographed Bridge of Sighs (1831), named after the even more famous structure in Venice. Cambridge's

Bridge of Sighs, which Queen Victoria described in her diary as the most 'pretty and picturesque' feature of the University, symbolises a new spirit of expansion, connecting the old part of St John's College with the first development to take place on the marshy west side of the river south of Magdalene Street. Until the 1820s, the Cam provided a natural western boundary for the University, separating it from the meadows beyond; but faced with demands for extra accommodation St John's took a step across the river and commissioned the extensive neo-gothic New Court (1825–31). The buildings, with their elaborate central lantern known as The Wedding-Cake and covered walkway evoking the ancient university streets of Padua or Bologna, paved the way for further expansion westward. To our right the old brick ranges (with dates of construction, 1624 and 1671, on their gables) dip into the waters of the river in a manner reminiscent of Bruges or Venice, while to our left a route through the cloisters of New Court arrives at the modernist Cripps Building of 1963–7. This extensive residential complex leads at its far north-western end to the so-called School of Pythagoras, a late twelfth-century stone building on two storeys with Norman arches which has no connection with the ancient Greek mathematician but which is said to be one of the oldest surviving houses in England. A sizeable dwelling in Norman terms, it is now used for drama, concerts, and other events. This and the neighbouring Merton Hall, a timber-framed range dating from Tudor times, are owned by St John's.

SELWYN DIVINITY SCHOOL

Tracking back to St John's Street, we find opposite St John's gatehouse the neo-gothic Divinity School (1878–9), founded by and named after the Lady Margaret Professor of Divinity William Selwyn (brother of the G. A. Selwyn commemorated by Selwyn College), and built by Basil Champneys in red brick with stone dressing. The original Divinity School of c.1400 (now part of the Old Schools) was the centre of the University; and the central location of this successor indicates the continuing importance of the study of theology and related subjects at Cambridge.

Near this site until 1865 stood the medieval Church of All Saints, whose churchyard now forms a triangle bordered by All Saints' Passage where craft stallholders frequently ply their wares.

ROUND CHURCH (HOLY SEPULCHRE)

Opposite the northern end of St John's Street we find one of only about 11 early round churches surviving in England (though there are records of 23). The shape dates back to the time of the first Christians, who built circular structures around sepulchres or tombs as a symbolic way of protecting and highlighting their contents. In Jerusalem the rotunda of the Church of the Holy Sepulchre of Christ was seen by crusading knights who made their way from Norman Europe to the Holy Land and returned to preserve the tradition of round-church building in their native lands. Cambridge's version was put up shortly after 1130 by a small order of canons regular and dedicated to the Holy Sepulchre. Inside, the Round Church retains the form of its original Norman ambulatory, with eight columns and arches in a rather tight circle featuring decorative carving, much of the actual detail dating from restoration during the nineteenth century. The building had been altered and extended to the east in the 1400s, with the addition of gothic windows, a polygonal lantern, and wooden angels which survive in the chancel and north aisle; but was considerably modified and enlarged again in 1841 by Anthony Salvin, who restored to it a turreted roof and rounded windows, and who built a new belltower which can be seen outside to the north east of the main rotunda.

UNION SOCIETY

Convened during its early years in rooms at the back of an inn, the Cambridge Union Society moved in 1866 to a purpose-built terracotta and red-brick structure characteristic of its architect Alfred Waterhouse, lying at the end of a path beside the Round Church.

Founded in 1815, the Society is the University debating club where budding politicians and other public figures have tested their speaking skills. The Union has a President, who sits during debates on a dais and observes the speakers who are given the floor on one or other side of him. An audience of students and other members votes (like members of the British parliament) by walking through the 'Ayes' or the 'Noes' door to show which side of the debate has persuaded them. Presidents of the Union have included William Whewell, John Maynard Keynes, R. A. Butler, Archbishop Michael Ramsey, and Norman St John Stevas. A regular cycle of debates still takes place in the traditional manner each week during term.

23 *The Round Church.*

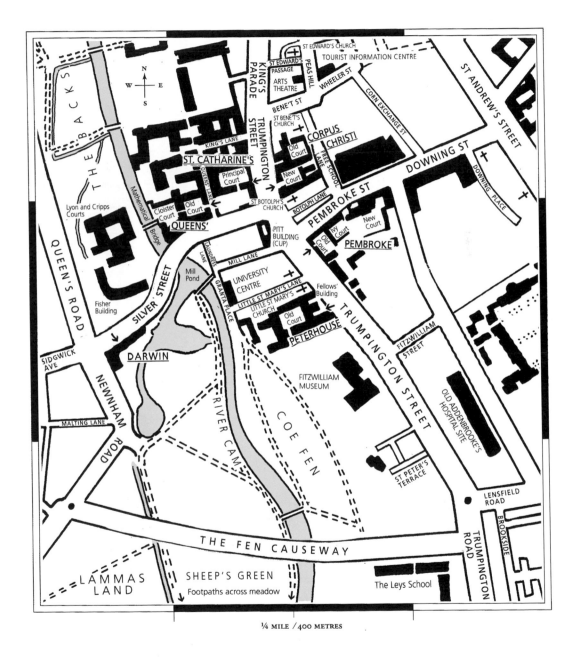

Arrows ➔ indicate the usual tourist entrance to each college.

ST EDWARD'S CHURCH

The Church of St Edward occupies an attractively secluded square surrounded by antiquarian bookshops, accessible via a passage just to the north west of the Tourist Information Centre near Market Hill. It dates from 1400, with earlier traces including the lower west tower of c.1200, and contains spacious chancel aisles added in 1446 to accommodate worshipping members from Clare and Trinity Hall. Both colleges had previously made use of the Church of St John Zachary which was demolished during the site-clearance resulting from Henry VI's foundation of King's. From 1523 to 1525 leading Protestant reformers including Hugh Latimer held meetings at a nearby inn, and preached in St Edward's from a linenfold-panelled pulpit of 1510 which survives in the church.

The neighbouring market place is much smaller than it was in medieval times, when St Edward's would have stood at the edge of a vast expanse of stalls stretching as far as the churches of Holy Trinity and St Andrew's to the east.

ARTS THEATRE

On Peas Hill opposite the Tourist Information Centre stands Cambridge's Arts Theatre, opened in 1936 by a group of drama enthusiasts including the great economist John Maynard Keynes, who was a fellow of King's College. Margot Fonteyn danced here on the opening night. Among those using the theatre over the years have been the Cambridge Footlights, the revue group which has produced a string of famous entertainers including Jonathan Miller, John Cleese, Eric Idle, Clive James, Stephen Fry, and Emma Thompson.

ST BENE'T'S CHURCH

This Anglo-Saxon church (dedicated to St Bene't or Benedict) stood before a University ever existed in Cambridge, when much of the land between here and the river was a wet marsh. The rough-hewn tower is the oldest building fabric in the county of Cambridgeshire, revealing the relatively basic architectural techniques characteristic of English builders before the Norman conquest of 1066. Blocks of rubble have been piled together with a rough mortar, protected by neater quoins or cornerstones

24 *Tower of St Bene't's Church: the oldest surviving building in Cambridgeshire.*

which alternate horizontally and vertically all the way up the sides of the tower to keep frost and damp out of the vulnerable angles where the side walls join. The twin-apertures in the top section are Saxon windows, low and narrow to avoid undermining the strength of the structure.

Inside, the much-restored gothic nave retains at its west end a splendid Saxon tower arch, heavy pillars surmounted by worn carvings of beasts (this work dating from *c.*1000). A plaque on the north wall of the tower commemorates Fabian Stedman, born in 1633, who developed the art of change-ringing using the bells in this tower.

St Bene't's originally housed priests who ministered to the inhabitants of a modest river-trading town and witnessed, in the early thirteenth century, the first bands of scholars congregating around its precincts. With the growth of the college system the scholars took over, and in 1352 the new Corpus Christi College adopted St Bene't's as its chapel, a status the church retained until 1579.

CORPUS CHRISTI COLLEGE

Entered from Trumpington Street, this second smallest of the central colleges is (like the smallest, Peterhouse) historically among the most interesting. It was founded in 1352 by two citizens' guilds, and although one of the guilds was headed by the Duke of Lancaster, Corpus Christi was regarded as having broken the medieval pattern of foundation by wealthy aristocrats, clerics, or royal officials – and is indeed the only civic foundation of its kind in Cambridge or Oxford. The college's symbol, a pelican plucking her own breast to feed her young, represents Christ's bodily sacrifice: the emblem may be seen on a shield in the vault of the gateway and in prominent places around the college. Despite its close connection with the citizens of Cambridge, Corpus Christi was nonetheless an early victim of 'town–gown' tensions, and in 1381 a mob of townspeople raided its precincts and burned its charters, in protest at rents levied on them by the college to pay for its upkeep.

Passing into the harmonious New Court (1823–7 by William Wilkins), we see a long neo-gothic library range standing to our right, which contains one of the country's most important collections of medieval books and manuscripts. Many were left by Matthew Parker, who was Master of the college from 1544 and especially influential as Archbishop of Canterbury under Elizabeth I. While in favour of Henry VIII's Reformation of the Church, Parker was a man of strong antiquarian tastes who salvaged numerous manuscripts and books from the despoiled monasteries.

Opposite the main entrance to the nineteenth-century court a chapel is centrally placed; and the architect Wilkins (whose most famous building was the National Gallery in London) chose to be buried here.

Leaving the court by a passageway in the north-east corner we encounter a more ancient scene. The Old Court of Corpus Christi is indeed the oldest surviving residential range in Cambridge or Oxford, and gives an excellent idea of the atmosphere of a small college during the great wave of early collegiate foundations in the mid-1300s. The buildings round this court have been subsequently expanded, with buttresses and dormer windows added, but the basic fabric (of rubble with clunch facing), the tracery round the lower windows, and the essential shape and size, remain as they were not long after 1352. A plaque on the far wall commemorates the residence in this court of Christopher Marlowe and John Fletcher, leading playwrights of the Elizabethan age and contemporaries of Shakespeare. It is remarkable to reflect that these rooms were already 200 years old by the time Marlowe and Fletcher inhabited them.

A much later literary association was struck up at Corpus Christi when writers Christopher Isherwood (*Goodbye to Berlin*, 1939) and Edward Upward (*Journey to the Border*, 1938) became close friends as undergraduates here.

The passageway in the north-west corner of Old Court was the entrance to the college until the nineteenth century; then as now, it led to the Anglo-Saxon Church of St Bene't, which the original Corpus Christi took as its chapel. In the later fifteenth century a brick corridor was erected to connect the college with the church and for many years Corpus Christi was known unofficially as Bene't College.

ST CATHARINE'S COLLEGE

The saint whose name is commemorated by the college on Trumpington Street opposite Corpus Christi is clear from the golden Catharine Wheel surmounting its front gates:

St Catharine (the patron saint of scholars) was put to death on a wheel. St Catharine's Hall was established here in 1473 with money provided by the Provost of King's, its larger northern neighbour. It changed its name in 1860, as had Clare in 1856, from 'Hall' to 'College', and its spelling distinguishes it from St Catherine's College in Oxford. The college is known colloquially as 'Cats'.

As also at Clare, the medieval site was cleared in the seventeenth century to make way for a grander four-sided court in the classical style by the Grumbold family of masons. Owing to a shortage of money only three sides were completed, leaving the refreshingly open layout which now recedes from the street and gives an impression of depth (in contrast with the

25 *Old Court, Corpus Christi College.*

26 *St Catharine's College, looking into Principal Court.*

gothic fronts of the other colleges hereabouts), broken only by the well-proportioned gateposts, iron gates, and railings dating from 1779. The chapel on the north side of the lawn is modelled on Christopher Wren's work at Pembroke College; and contains the remains, marked by a black slab on the antechapel floor, of Dr John Addenbrooke, a bursar of St Catharine's who died in 1719 leaving money for the foundation of the Cambridge hospital which now bears his name.

Fronting Trumpington Street north of the entrance to St Catharine's (just before the point where the road formally becomes King's Parade) is a college building with first-floor railings which used to be the Bull Inn, a hotel popular with American servicemen during the Second World War; and an archway where Thomas Hobson, the University 'carrier', had his stables from 1570 to 1630. Hobson's job was to rent horses to travellers making the journey to London – travellers who always wanted the best and fastest horses, with the result that these animals were always tired. The carrier devised a strict rotation system where each horse arriving from a journey went to the back of the queue, so that travellers seeking a horse took the next one in line. This became known as 'Hobson's choice' – i.e. no choice at all – a phrase which entered the language on this spot. Behind the archway today, on either side of King's Lane, lies a well-concealed warren of modern buildings (including an underground car park) paid for jointly by St Catharine's and King's Colleges, whose sites the narrow lane divides. This is the only instance in 700 years of a single architectural scheme linking two Cambridge colleges.

Even more recently (1976–81) Cats invested in an impressive new residential site, St Chad's, in west Cambridge where West Road meets Grange Road, helping it into the top ten colleges in terms of student numbers. An honorary fellow is violinist Yehudi Menuhin, who in 1973 led an orchestral celebration of the five-hundredth anniversary of the foundation.

ST BOTOLPH'S CHURCH

St Botolph is the patron saint of travellers, and churches dedicated to him are often found at the entrances to towns. The word 'Boston' is a contraction of 'Botolph's Town', applied first to the port of Boston in Lincolnshire and adopted later by Boston, Massachusetts. At a junction of medieval Cambridge (near where Silver Street now joins Trumpington Street) stood the city gates admitting the road from London, next to a church which has existed in much its present form since 1400, with nave and aisles dating from before 1350. Items of interest inside St Botolph's Church include the elaborate octagonal font cover of 1637, a remnant of the taste for decoration encouraged in those years by Archbishop William Laud.

PITT BUILDING

Diagonally opposite St Botolph's a large gothic-towered structure, known playfully as the 'Freshers' Church' due to its resemblance in the eyes of new undergraduates to a church building, is in fact the Pitt Building, headquarters of the Cambridge University Press. In the Oriel Room jutting towards the street at first-floor level, the Press (whose bookshop we have seen at 1 Trinity Street) hosts meetings of the University Press Syndicate at which decisions are taken on the 1,500 or so new books and the many journals published from here each year. The building (1831–3) was named after British Prime Minister William Pitt the Younger, and housed printing and publishing staff until the Press moved first printing (1963) and then

27 *Tudor lodge, Queens' College, seen across Cloister Court.*

publishing (1980) to its spacious modern site near the railway station. The University Printing Services (a jobbing printing factory for the University and colleges) now occupies most of the premises.

QUEENS' COLLEGE

Founded in 1448 next to a Carmelite friary, Queens' is best approached from Queens' Lane (off Silver Street). This was the former Milne Street, one of the central routes through medieval Cambridge, and the fine red-brick gatehouse can be imagined fronting an important thoroughfare. The college is named after two queens (Margaret of Anjou, wife of Henry VI; and Elizabeth Woodville, wife of Edward IV), its plural title nowadays distinguishing it from The (singular) Queen's College in Oxford (named after Philippa, wife of Edward III).

The Cambridge foundation owes its origins to a priest called Andrew Dokett, vicar of nearby St Botolph's Church, who enlisted the support of these early royal patrons. The worn keystone on the outer side of the gate is thought to represent Dokett holding the college's founding charter.

The gate and court behind it (1440s) represent the first use of brick as a building material on this scale in collegiate Cambridge, and remain one of the best examples of medieval red-brick architecture in Britain. This too is Cambridge's most perfect surviving execution of the college courtyard concept derived in part from the monastic model, with kitchens, hall, parlour, residential quarters, library, chapel (now part of the library), and gate built into a compact square, private and inward-looking. The red-brick court scheme, adopted later at St John's (whose founding father John Fisher had been President of Queens'), is one of the particular glories of Cambridge.

North of Old Court is the newer college

chapel, a good example of late Victorian church building by G. F. Bodley, with a priceless altar triptych by a Flemish artist of the late fifteenth century.

The medieval dining hall in the west range of Old Court has been enlarged and embellished in subsequent years, notably by the stately neo-classical screens (1732–4), the decorated roof (1875), and the fireplace with overmantel featuring tiles designed by Pre-Raphaelite artists and made by William Morris's company. Screens shielding a window in the middle of the passage may be opened to provide a good view. Records survive of eating arrangements in the old hall – and until 1831, with students getting up rather earlier than today, dinner was scheduled for 3 pm.

Moving west from Old Court, we reach the most attractive of Cambridge's small courtyards, Cloister Court. This was an extension of the original premises, incorporating a covered cloister walk, and in the late sixteenth century the striking Tudor lodge with its upper gallery was added to provide more room for a resident Master (known here as a President) and his guests. Its wooden beams, plaster, and jutting bay windows appealingly complement the cloister ranges of medieval brick. The contrast between the cloister and the lodge catches a moment of transition between the relatively simple, communal character of medieval life and the domestic splendours of the Tudor age. The head of a college would have to entertain royalty or aristocracy – indeed Catherine of Aragon is said to have stayed at Queens' back in 1519, Cardinal Wolsey in 1520 – and facilities were required to cater for the increasingly opulent tastes of the upper classes.

The most famous lodger at Queens' was probably Desiderius Erasmus, the humanist scholar,

classicist, and theologian, who came to Cambridge from his native Rotterdam and, according to oral tradition, chose the college as a base during his four-year stay (1510–14). Erasmus is said to have prepared his edition of the Greek New Testament here. He recorded his impression of Cambridge in letters to a friend, complaining that 'I cannot go out of doors because of the plague ... I am beset with thieves, and the wine is no better than vinegar ... I do not like the ale of this place at all ...'

28 *Mathematical Bridge connecting the old and new parts of Queens' College, near Silver Street, during a river flood.*

From Silver Street, where the road crosses the river, the Queens' Mathematical Bridge, built originally in 1749 by James Essex, may be viewed. The present version (1904) is the third on the site to be constructed to an identical design. The building on the corner immediate- ly to our right is also by Essex, and beyond it overlooking Silver Street at the bend in the road is the small tower where Erasmus is reput- ed to have lived. The west range of Cloister Court stretches downriver, in medieval brick with gothic window recesses (1460s). To the left a more recent red-brick structure, the Fisher Building (1935–6), swings round the corner, bordering to its north a large modern development consisting of Cripps and Lyon Courts, built in stages over the last 20 years.

DARWIN COLLEGE

Founded in 1964 and achieving collegiate status in 1965, Darwin, at the western end of Silver Street, was the first modern Cambridge college designed solely for postgraduates. Unlike Oxford (whose All Souls survived from the Middle Ages as a college devoted to higher-level study), Cambridge had no such institution remaining. The establishment was funded by three older colleges (Trinity, St John's, and Caius), partly in order to relieve their own increasing postgraduate load and partly in response to a recognised shortage of places in Cambridge for postgraduate students. A picturesque site was found at the southern end of the Backs in houses lately vacated by the Darwin family (descendants of famous naturalist Charles Darwin), which gave its name to the new graduate institution – the first Cambridge college to accept both men and women. The Victorian buildings have been tastefully augmented in a development flanking a leafy byway of the River Cam, just above the Mill Pond.

Darwin has by a large margin the highest number of postgraduate students (about 500) of any college in the University. Overseas students drawn from over 50 countries make up half of its membership.

UNIVERSITY CENTRE

Laundress Lane joins Silver Street to Mill Lane, where the Mill Pond is a popular base for punters, whose escapades can be viewed from adjacent lawns. On Granta Place, the concrete-framed University Centre (1964–7), affectionately known as the 'Grad. Pad' (reflecting its origin in the old Graduates' Club), provides eating and entertainment facilities overlooking the river for graduate students, visiting scholars, senior members of the University, and University staff.

PEMBROKE COLLEGE

Opposite the other end of Mill Lane stands the third oldest of the colleges, founded in 1347 by Marie de Valence, widow of the Earl of Pembroke, a wealthy lady descended from the royal families of both England and France. Like other aristocratic women before and after her, she considered the foundation of a

college of learning a worthwhile use of her money, endowing it (originally under the name Pembroke Hall) with generous sums. The bicycles of Pembroke students are identified by a letter 'V' for Valence.

Pembroke was the college of the great poet Edmund Spenser, author of *The Faerie Queene*, who came to study here in 1569. Modern Poet Laureate Ted Hughes was an undergraduate from 1951 to 1954, as was comedian Peter Cook from 1957 to 1960. Australian writer and entertainer Clive James read English at Pembroke in the 1960s, and has recalled his Cambridge experiences in the memoir *May Week was in June* (1990). The college offers good examples of various architectural styles over 600 years and retains a lived-in feel which some of the neater and prettier colleges lack. Its chapel launched the career of that most famous of English architects, Christopher Wren.

Before crossing the busy junction where Pembroke Street joins Trumpington Street, it is worth pausing to study the various sections of wall along the southern side of Pembroke Street, built shortly after the foundation of the college in 1347. Newly cleaned, the lighter section beginning a short distance along the street reveals the clunchwork as it might have looked in those early years. The brick building nearest the corner is the Old Library, originally the chapel, and one of the first college chapels to be built in Cambridge.

Christopher Wren took up architecture in his thirties having already made a career as a Professor of Astronomy at Oxford. Designed in 1663 and opened in 1665, Pembroke Chapel was his first completed building and one of the first classical-style churches in England. Its stone west front overlooks Trumpington Street, framed by Corinthian pilasters and surmounted by a hexagonal lantern; the entrance can be reached via a covered cloister (added later) to the right of the porter's lodge inside Old Court. Wren left the brickwork exposed on the court side (the building was extended eastwards in 1880 by the younger George Gilbert Scott). Like its exterior, the chapel interior observes the strict mathematical proportions that were a hallmark of Wren's early classicism. An ornately plastered ceiling of 1690 crowns the work, offset to the east by Scott's heavy but not out-of-place marble columns.

A passageway leads past the Victorian dining hall into Ivy Court, containing architecture contemporary with Wren (who sent his son to the college in 1691). On the south side of the court there is a coat-of-arms above the window of the first-floor rooms occupied by the poet Thomas Gray from 1756 until his death in 1771; the college possesses the autograph of his 'An Elegy in a Country Churchyard'. The same rooms were occupied by William Pitt the Younger, who became an undergraduate in 1773 before his fifteenth birthday and Prime Minister shortly before his twenty-fifth.

Another arch gives access to the leafy precincts of New Court, with Library Court, containing the distinctive turret and clock of Alfred Waterhouse's library, and a statue of Pitt, behind to the right at the southern end of the site. These larger buildings are all evidence of the extraordinarily rapid expansion of Pembroke in the Victorian period, during which time it became known more commonly by the name 'College' than 'Hall'. Earlier, the walk through the gardens had been loved by Protestant martyr Nicholas Ridley, Master of the college, who in his farewell to it from prison, soon before his martyrdom in 1555, recalls learning much of St Paul's and other Epistles by heart in the orchard.

Pembroke is now a medium-sized college with a total of about 500 students.

LITTLE ST MARY'S CHURCH

This church was once known as St Peter's, a name it gave to Peterhouse, the college with which it is linked by a gallery to the south. Although re-consecrated in honour of the Virgin Mary in 1352, the new St Mary the Less retained a connection with Peterhouse, serving as its college chapel until 1632. The east window facing Trumpington Street is a particularly fine example of the flowing tracery of the decorated gothic period, dating from the rebuilding of the church (1340–52). Inside, there is a tablet to former vicar of the parish Godfrey Washington (1670–1729), a great uncle of the first President of the United States whose family arms of stars, stripes, and an eagle, carved here in 1736, were adapted in 1776 for the American flag and crest. A delightful churchyard at the back, somewhat overgrown, adjoins the north-facing wall of Peterhouse with its medieval stone and brickwork.

Beside the churchyard, Little St Mary's Lane contains, like Botolph Lane and Portugal Place elsewhere in the city centre, rows of attractive house frontages preserving their original line.

31 (top) *Peterhouse dining hall, seen across Old Court.*

32 (bottom) *The west front of Peterhouse Chapel.*

PETERHOUSE

In 1984 Peterhouse, the oldest of the colleges, celebrated its seven-hundredth anniversary. It is also the smallest college situated in central Cambridge, with just over 300 students.

The establishment of Merton College in Oxford, finalised in 1274, had provided a precedent for a group of scholars sharing premises under a set of governing statutes which allowed them a more co-ordinated existence in the service of scholarship. In 1280 the Bishop of Ely set up a foundation in the precincts of St John's Hospital, Cambridge (where St John's College now stands) and in 1284 it moved to its own site next to the Church of St Peter (now called Little St Mary's), whose name it took, along with a royal charter (1285) establishing it with an independent identity similar to that of Merton. The mode of life thus established, centring on the key concepts of lodging, library, and dining room, still dominates Cambridge (now with 31 colleges) seven centuries later.

Peterhouse (never known as Peterhouse College, though often in the eighteenth and early nineteenth centuries referred to as St Peter's College) retains traces of its original thirteenth-century buildings, visible around the southern doorway of the old hall and reached via a passageway between the hall and kitchens on the south side of Old Court. These stone walls, much embellished and extended in later years, are the earliest surviving college building fabric in Cambridge. The hall is better viewed from the north where its later oriel window, ashlar, and lantern dominate Old Court. Despite the alterations, we may imagine a hall on something like this scale, the very first of its kind in Cambridge, accommodating daily groups of dining scholars 700 years ago as it still does today.

Into its small eastern court Peterhouse fits three important buildings: the chapel, extending almost to the street; north of it, the neoclassical Fellows' (or Burrough's) Building; and, flush with the street at the porter's lodge end, the red-brick Perne Library (1593–c.1640). The Fellows' Building (1738–42) is a sedate structure in the Palladian style, housing senior members and designed by James Burrough. The poet Thomas Gray, who had a paranoid fear of fire, lived on the top floor and had a metal bracket fixed outside his window (it can still be seen on the north side), supporting a strap to lower himself to the ground in the event of a conflagration. Provoked by an incident in which a fellow-lodger taunted him by shouting 'Fire!', and feeling that he lacked sympathetic friends in Peterhouse, Gray moved across the road to Pembroke College in 1756.

Peterhouse Chapel (1628–32) has, at either end, a gothic window, classical pediment, and baroque scrolls, reflecting the taste of the Masters who sponsored and completed it, Matthew Wren (uncle of Christopher) and John Cosin. At a time when Puritanism, with its plain, simple style, was in the ascendant, Wren and Cosin controversially upheld 'high church' conventions such as the burning of incense, bowing to the altar, and lighting of candles before a crucifix.

More recently, Peterhouse was a pioneer among the colleges in installing electric light. This was arranged for the six-hundredth anniversary celebrations in 1884 by Lord Kelvin, the physicist who gave his name to the absolute scale of temperature. Kelvin was a fellow here, as are Frank Whittle, the inventor of the jet engine, and Max Perutz, John Kendrew,

and Aaron Klug, all Nobel Prize winners in Molecular Biology. Peterhouse has been the home of novelist Kingsley Amis, who taught English here in the early 1960s. Women were admitted as undergraduates in 1985, and the first woman fellow was appointed in the same year. Although the college's name was adapted for the title of a well-known satirical novel about Cambridge life, *Porterhouse Blue* (1974), the book's author, Tom Sharpe, was actually an undergraduate at Pembroke, and his satire is not based on any particular college.

Across the street from the porter's lodge, behind a wall and an ornate gate, an elegant three-storeyed town house of 1702, with warm, light-red brickwork, was bequeathed to Peterhouse by its builder and is used to accommodate the college's fortunate Master during his term in office. Recent Masters have included eminent historian Hugh Trevor-Roper (Lord Dacre), who lived here from 1980 to 1987 and who formed part of a distinguished tradition of historical studies in the college also represented by Herbert Butterfield, Denis Brogan, and David Knowles.

By the kerb outside Peterhouse, visitors should be careful not to step into 'Hobson's conduit', a channel cut along the side of the road which was designed originally in the early seventeenth century to carry fresh water to the city from the hills to the south, and sponsored by University carrier Thomas Hobson. The elaborate fountain-head, which was in the middle of the market place between 1614 and 1856, now stands as a monument to Hobson where Trumpington Street joins Lensfield Road.

FITZWILLIAM MUSEUM

The Fitzwilliam is the principal museum of the University of Cambridge and contains an

33 *Fitzwilliam Museum.*

internationally important collection of paintings, antiquities, and other artefacts. Opened in 1848, it is funded both by the University and by special endowments and trusts. Many of its treasures have been bequeathed over the years, and the museum takes its name from its first benefactor, the Seventh Viscount Fitzwilliam of Merrion, whose gift to the University of £100,000 was received in 1816. Another eminent early patron was the writer and art critic John Ruskin, who in 1861 gave 25 watercolours by J. M. W. Turner. The imposing neo-classical Founder's Building with its gigantic portico and steps rising above the street was built between 1837 and 1875.

Among the treasures which today attract scholars and visitors from around the world are a range of the best works by William Blake; one of the foremost existing collections of prints by Rembrandt; extensive holdings of Greek, Roman, and especially medieval coins; paintings including Domenico Veneziano's *The Annunciation*, Titian's *Tarquin and Lucretia*, Veronese's *Hermes, Herse and Aglauros*, and others by Rubens, van Dyck, Poussin, Claude, Hogarth, Reynolds, Gainsborough, Stubbs, Turner, Constable, and Delacroix; drawings by Verrocchio, Leonardo, Watteau, Ingres, and Picasso; and exhibits of vases, ceramics, sculpture, portrait miniatures, and manuscripts.

A series of first-class exhibitions may be visited at the Fitzwilliam Museum, supplementing the permanent collection, and there is a well-stocked bookshop.

OLD ADDENBROOKE'S HOSPITAL SITE

Slightly to the south of the Fitzwilliam Museum, on a site lying back from the east side of Trumpington Street and now thoroughly re-developed by the University, stood the original Addenbrooke's Hospital. Constructed in 1740 with funds left by Dr John Addenbrooke, a physician of St Catharine's College, the hospital survived here until modern times when it was removed to its present position two miles further south, where Hills Road heads out of urban Cambridge. One of the country's foremost teaching and research hospitals, and among the largest hospital complexes in Europe, the new Addenbrooke's houses the University's School of Clinical Medicine, and has led the way in many medical developments of recent years. The old site is now home to the Graduate Union, Olivetti Research, the Research Centre for English and Applied Linguistics, and the Judge Institute of Management Studies.

34 (top) *Addenbrooke's Hospital, Trumpington Street, in 1870. The Victorian façade was remodelled in 1931 and again in the mid-1990s.*

35 (bottom) *The Judge Institute of Management Studies, the latest manifestation of the Trumpington Street site. The Institute was opened by the Queen, in the presence of benefactor Sir Paul Judge, in March 1996.*

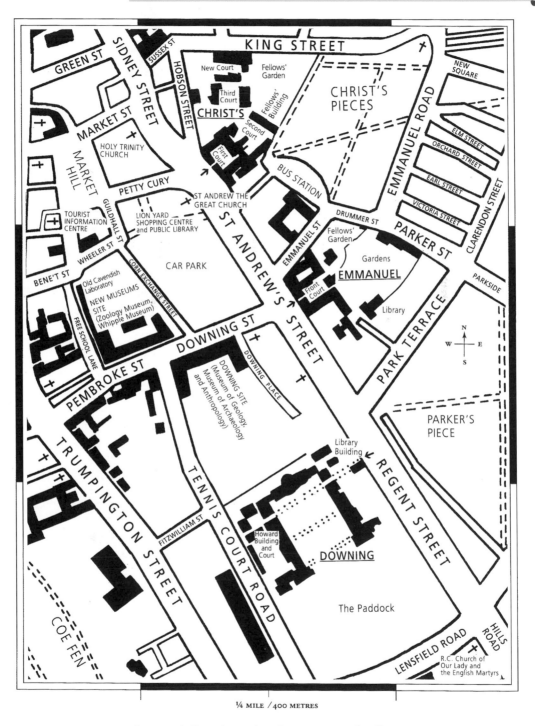

¼ MILE / 400 METRES

Arrows → indicate the usual tourist entrance to each college.

FREE SCHOOL LANE
AND NEW MUSEUMS SITE

Free School Lane runs south from Bene't Street and offers, from a point just in front of the Old Cavendish Laboratory, a fine perspective on medieval Cambridge. Here we look across the eastern range of Corpus Christi College's Old Court, where the ancient walls of the original lodgings stand back from the street. Behind these windows students have lived continuously for 650 years; and above them, beyond the roof, the tower of St Bene't's (c.1000) reaches back even further into history. Free School Lane is named after the Perse School (now located on Hills Road) which was opened here in 1618 by a bequest of Stephen Perse of Caius College.

The Old Cavendish Laboratory, founded by William Cavendish, Seventh Duke of Devonshire, is commemorated by a plaque on the wall behind us. In 1874 Cambridge's pioneer laboratory of experimental physics was established in these Victorian buildings, which for the next 100 years would witness a series of important events in the fields of physics and molecular biology. Here in 1897 J. J. Thomson discovered the electron, and in 1919 his most famous pupil, Ernest Rutherford, returned to the Cavendish to pursue his studies of the composition of the atom, which would prove crucial to the development of nuclear physics. Here in 1932 James Chadwick discovered the neutron. And here in 1953 Francis Crick and James Watson produced their famous paper suggesting for the first time that the double-helix structure of DNA might provide a mechanism whereby genetic material could be copied from cell to cell and generation to generation, thus giving rise to modern genetic engineering. The work of these laboratories has now removed to larger sites, but the Old Cavendish building remains as a monument to such scientific breakthroughs and to no fewer than 22 Nobel Prize winners between 1904 and 1973.

Near the Cavendish plaque an archway leads during University business hours to the New Museums Site, a cluster of buildings where until the 1840s the Botanic Garden lay. The middle of the nineteenth century saw rapid developments in the study of science, and the University of Cambridge led the way. The term 'scientist' was coined by a Cambridge Professor, William Whewell, in 1833, and Natural Sciences became part of the

36 *St Bene't's Church seen from Free School Lane above the outer eastern range of Corpus Christi College's Old Court.*

University curriculum under his guidance, winning approval in 1851. The forward-looking leadership of Albert, the Prince Consort, who was Chancellor of the University from 1847 to 1861, facilitated the pace of change, as did a Royal Commission of 1850 which investigated the function of the ancient universities and resulted in new statutes for Cambridge. New disciplines such as geology and zoology began to emerge, inspired by the work of thinkers like Adam Sedgwick, the pioneer geologist who also battled for liberal reforms (such as the abolition of religious 'tests' limiting degrees to Anglicans) within the University; and his pupil Charles Darwin, who had been an undergraduate in Cambridge. Between 1863 and 1914 the land to the east of Free School Lane was increasingly filled with buildings housing science faculties and laboratories, and this remains the hub of scientific Cambridge.

Inside the Free School Lane entrance, the Mond Building (1932) just to our right accommodates a modern institution: the University Department of Aerial Photography, which has a major collection of air photographs covering most of Great Britain. Here visitors may consult the archives and look at particular aerial perspectives of their own region. A crocodile cut into the curved brick surface to the right of the doors is the work of English sculptor and engraver Eric Gill, commissioned by his friend, the distinguished Soviet physicist Peter Kapitza, to commemorate Ernest Rutherford.

37 *Old Cavendish Laboratory: an elementary science class, before 1911. Reproduced from* A History of the Cavendish Laboratory 1871–1910 *(1910).*

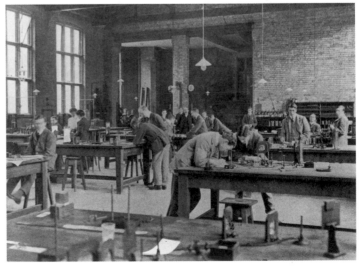

The site also houses the University Computer Laboratory, near the Babbage Lecture Hall named after Charles Babbage (1792–1871), the pioneer computer scientist who was Lucasian Professor of Mathematics here. In 1993 Cambridge became one of the first universities to join SuperJANET, the high-speed national computer network making use of the latest fibre-optic technology. Back on Free School Lane, a plaque further south designates the old Engineering Laboratory (1899), with its stepped gable.

At the end of the lane Botolph House leans rather precariously to the east: evidence of the King's Ditch, a defensive channel which surrounded the medieval town and which was probably dug before 1066. It survives here beneath the building's foundations.

WHIPPLE MUSEUM OF THE HISTORY OF SCIENCE

Nearby on Free School Lane, beneath an arch proclaiming the former Laboratory of Physical Chemistry, lies the entrance to one of the top five museums of its kind in the country. Robert Stuart Whipple (former chairman of the Cambridge Scientific Instrument Company, which had been founded by Charles Darwin's son Horace) gave his private collection of scientific instruments to the University in 1944, inaugurating an archive which is now part of the Department of History and Philosophy of Science. Dating mainly from the sixteenth to nineteenth centuries, the display items include early mathematical instruments such as astrolabes and sundials, navigation and surveying equipment, electrical measuring instruments, astronomical telescopes, microscopes (including one owned by Charles Darwin), spectroscopes, and balances. Equipment from the Old Cavendish Laboratory is

38 The Cambridge emblem (Alma Mater Cantabrigia, a nude female figure with flowing milk who bears a sun, castle, and chalice) and motto ('Hinc Lucem et Pocula Sacra', exhorting students to drink from the fount of light, wisdom, and knowledge). These are seen above the archway leading to the Downing Site, Downing Street, with a date of 1903 indicating the beginning of an important period of development for the University science faculties on this site.

displayed on the lower of the museum's two floors.

MUSEUM OF ZOOLOGY

To the east on Pembroke Street, the main entrance to the New Museums Site lies opposite the top of Tennis Court Road. On the site, diagonally across from this gateway, is a museum which has formed part of the University's Department of Zoology since 1938. The staff are active in University teaching and research. The displays are spaciously presented: a necessity in the case of the whale skeletons, which are among exhibits including skeletons of extinct birds such as Darwin's Rhea, and the fish he collected from his voyages on the *Beagle*. Two live reticulated pythons, representing the world's largest breed of snake, inhabit a case in the foyer.

39 *Adam Sedgwick (1785–1873): portrait by Lowes Dickenson (1867).*

DOWNING SITE

Downing Street is the eastern continuation of Pembroke Street. Between 1896 and 1902 Downing College sold sections of its land to the University, which needed more space to accommodate the fast-growing scientific component of its curriculum. The site now entered from Downing Street was developed between 1903 and 1939 and houses major science departments including those of Anatomy, Earth Sciences, Experimental Psychology, Genetics, and Plant Sciences.

MUSEUM OF ARCHAEOLOGY AND ANTHROPOLOGY

The Downing Site contains (to the right of the entrance) the Museum of Archaeology and Anthropology. Part of the Faculty of Archaeology and Anthropology, this originated in the 1880s, moving to its present site during the First World War. Its curatorial staff also teaches and undertakes research in the University. Part of the collection focuses on local antiquities, and finds from the East Anglian area (particularly from the Anglo-Saxon period) are displayed in quantity. However, items from a range of cultures past and present are contained in this well laid-out building, including weapons, tools, totem poles, tribal masks, and grave relics.

SEDGWICK MUSEUM OF GEOLOGY

To the left of the Downing Site entrance, at the top of the steps, is a museum named after nineteenth-century scientist Adam Sedgwick (1785–1873), containing one of the world's lead-ing fossil collections, as well as dinosaur skeletons, and the oldest intact collection of geological relics, which belonged to John Woodward (1665–1728). This collector also gave his name to the Woodwardian Professorship of Geology in Cambridge, held in the nineteenth century by Sedgwick, who inaugurated the teaching of geology in the University and counted Charles Darwin among his students. In 1859 Darwin sent his former professor a copy of his The Origin of Species, causing Sedgwick, who cannot have thought that this would become one of the most influential works ever written, to reply: 'I have read your book with more pain than pleasure. Parts of it I admired greatly, parts I laughed at till my sides were almost sore; other parts I read with absolute sorrow, because I think them utterly false and grievously mischievous.'

The museum is now part of the University's Department of Earth Sciences.

DOWNING COLLEGE

Built on a 15-acre site, Downing is the most spacious of the central colleges, its vast lawns stretching away from the neo-classical fore-court affording an unexpected impression of grandeur when entered via the claustrophobic bustle of Regent Street (the southern continuation of St Andrew's Street). This college was founded in 1800, with money provided for the purpose in the will of Sir George Downing, grandson of the man who built Downing Street, London residence of the British Prime Minister. Downing died in 1749, but legal wrangles over his will prevented its proper execution for 50 years. The foundation came after a very long lull, no new college having been established in Cambridge since Sidney Sussex in 1596.

The imposing buildings on three sides of the lawns are in the Greek classical style, and were begun by William Wilkins, who had travelled in Greece and was instrumental in the neo-classical revival of the early nineteenth century: his work at Downing was executed between 1807 and 1820. The north side of the court was finally closed off in 1953 with the building of the chapel. Work continues on the site, still faithful to Wilkins's style, and three major new buildings by Quinlan Terry are to be found near the west and east gates, striking attempts to preserve a classical idiom in modern Cambridge architecture. On the Tennis Court Road side the Howard Building (1987) is used as a centre for receptions, conferences, and entertainments, and the adjacent Howard Court (1994) is a residential building; while near the Regent Street gate the Library Building (1993) adopts a colonnaded portico fronting a symmetrical plan capped by an octagon recalling the Tower of the Winds in Athens. Symbols carved on the building's frieze

were selected by Downing's fellows to represent subjects studied in the library, including Modern Languages (a tower of Babel), English (a laurel wreath), History (an hour glass), Astronomy (a radio telescope), and Biology (a DNA double helix). The whole, like much else in Downing and in Cambridge at large, is built in rich Ketton stone.

The north-western corner of the courts, along

40 *Downing College: looking across to the chapel range from the north-west corner of the grounds.*

from the Howard Building, affords an inspiring view across Downing's Paddock. The prominent spire that sets off the southern end of the lawns belongs to the Roman Catholic Church of Our Lady and the English Martyrs (1885–90) on Hills Road.

Downing is perhaps most widely known in modern times as the college of F. R. Leavis, the influential literary critic.

EMMANUEL COLLEGE

On St Andrew's Street opposite the end of Downing Street we find Emmanuel College, whose Front Court, beyond the porter's lodge, presents one of the best perspectives in Cambridge. These wide arcades provide a vantage from which the façade of Christopher Wren's chapel (1666–79) appears in fine proportion on the other side of the lawn. A pediment with clock, lantern, and cupola rises above Corinthian columns and pilasters interspersed with swags and garlands. The baroque effect of the ornamental carving is kept in check by a neat row of windows at first-floor level, behind which a gallery runs across the entire width of the court, supported on the open arcade below. Square and circular motifs play off each other and the result is a well-balanced composition further enhanced in certain lights by the pale rosy glow on the Ketton stone brought by Wren from Northamptonshire. This was Wren's second project in Cambridge (after Pembroke Chapel) and he designed it in the same year (1666) that he witnessed the Great Fire of London and decided to pursue a full-time career as an architect, having previously distinguished himself as a scientist and Oxford professor.

Emmanuel College had been founded in 1584 on the site of a Dominican friary dissolved at Henry VIII's Reformation of the English Church, and from the start it was a severely Protestant establishment with an inclination towards Puritanism. A training-ground for young pastors and preachers of a Calvinist persuasion, it came under pressure during the conservative backlash led by Archbishop Laud in the 1630s, and many Emmanuel men sailed away to plant new colonies on the east coast of America where they could pursue their religion in their own way. More than 30 of the first 100

41 *Emmanuel College Chapel, by Christopher Wren.*

university graduates to settle in New England in the generation after the Pilgrim Fathers were from Emmanuel – among them John Harvard, who helped to endow a new educational establishment in Newtown, Massachusetts, which came to bear his name (he is commemorated by a plaque in the passage leading into the antechapel and by a stained glass window). The settlement's first pastor was Thomas Shepard, in whose honour (as another distinguished product of Emmanuel College) Newtown was re-named Cambridge. The figures in the chapel windows (1884) are designed to illuminate the continuity of church history and the part played in it by members of the college.

Passing from Front Court on the south side of the chapel the visitor reaches the extensive college gardens, landscaped to include a picturesque duckpond. This is in fact the fish-pond of the old friary, whose thirteenth-century boundary wall, now brick-clad, can be identified to the south, beyond the croquet and tennis lawns. There too is a large building of 1910, now the college library; and to the viewer's right a red-brick range erected in the 1630s to meet a rapid growth in student numbers. North of the duckpond a gate leads into the Fellows' Garden which contains some very fine trees: to the right, a 200-year-old oriental plane; directly ahead, a massive copper beech; and in front of it a small oak planted by the Queen to mark the college's four-hundredth anniversary. The garden also contains an outdoor swimming pool, concealed behind the trees on a site used for bathing since at least 1744.

Aside from the chapel, Emmanuel's best architecture belongs to the eighteenth century, including the Westmorland Building on the south side of Front Court (named after the Sixth Earl of Westmorland, a direct descendant of the college's founder Walter Mildmay), and the elegantly panelled dining hall (an adaptation by James Essex of what had been the original Dominicans' church), which may be seen via a door in the north-west corner. A passage leads beyond the hall into a further court containing at its far end the Old Library, which served as the college's first chapel and until 1930 as its library, and which retains its original oak screen.

CHRIST'S COLLEGE

The carved heraldry above Christ's College gateway on St Andrew's Street is almost identical to that of St John's, reminding us that the two colleges were founded at about the same time (Christ's in 1505, St John's in 1511) with benefactions from Lady Margaret Beaufort,

whose arms are represented here. The great royal lady (mother of Henry VII) died in 1509 between the two foundation dates, and Christ's has the distinction of having been launched by her in person: she even lived in the Master's lodge for a short time. Astute visitors will notice that the statue in a niche above the arch is of Lady Margaret herself, whereas the one at St John's is of St John. The broad oak doors beneath Christ's gateway, with their robust linenfold panelling, date from the later Tudor period towards the end of the sixteenth century. In contrast with the East Anglian and south-of-England orientation of many of the earlier colleges, it was ordained that Christ's should take a good proportion of its fellows and students from the north.

Inside we encounter First Court, decorated with flowers for all seasons and colourful even in winter. The court was built quickly (1505–11) in the flush of enthusiasm following Lady Margaret's foundation: in fact her money was being used to renovate and replace an ailing older college on the same site, God's House, established here in 1446. The architectural uniformity of the court belies its actual building history: the original Tudor clunch and brick walls are hidden behind eighteenth-century

42 *Beaufort arms carved beneath the oriel window of the Master's lodge in First Court, Christ's College. The foundress, Lady Margaret Beaufort, lodged here.*

stone facing and windows, while the prominent Tudor-gothic dining hall on the far side is largely a nineteenth-century replica – although the architect, George Gilbert Scott the younger, was careful to re-use old materials where he could. The wisteria-covered Master's lodge to the left of the hall retains a Tudor oriel window, with original carving, again of the Beaufort arms, beneath it.

Christ's chapel, entered to the left of the lodge, contains high-quality medieval stained glass in its north windows; a portrait of Lady Margaret on the west wall; an unusual window linking the chapel to the Master's lodge, used originally by the foundress to watch mass from her oratory; and a brass eagle lectern of the late fifteenth century, said to be the best of its date in the country.

Through a passage between the hall and the kitchens stands, on the far side of Second Court, the Fellows' Building of 1640–3, an important landmark in Cambridge architecture which inaugurated the taste for classical motifs that would culminate in the Senate-House 80 years later. The identity of the Christ's architect is unknown, but he combined triangular and rounded pediments (see for example the main doors, or the dormer windows jutting from the roof) in an alternating scheme, and framed the building at each corner with an ionic pilaster in a spirit reminiscent of the work of Inigo Jones in London but quite new to Cambridge. This Fellows' Building, along with the main court at Clare, is the most imposing seventeenth-century collegiate structure dating from the years before Christopher Wren came to do his work at Pembroke, Emmanuel, and Trinity.

43 *Fellows' Building seen from Second Court, Christ's College.*

Through the central archway may be seen the beautiful Fellows' Garden, in which poet John Milton, author of *Paradise Lost*, gained inspiration. Milton (known as the Lady of Christ's because of his youthful appearance) was an undergraduate here from 1625 to 1629 and took his MA in 1632. Another famous Christ's student was the author of *The Origin of Species*, Charles Darwin. He came here in 1827, was accommodated in lodgings now marked by a plaque outside Boots on Sidney Street, and later wrote that 'No pursuit at Cambridge was followed with nearly so much eagerness or gave me so much pleasure as collecting beetles.' South African statesman General Jan Smuts studied at Christ's in the early years of the twentieth century,

later becoming Chancellor of the University. Writer and physicist C. P. Snow, whose novel *The Masters* (1951) describes the intrigues of Cambridge college life, was a fellow here until his death in 1980.

Rounding the corner to the north we enter Third Court, with its nineteenth-century range adapting the design of the Fellows' Building. Beyond, the stepped layers of New Court (1966–70) give rise to its affectionate nickname The Typewriter Building. Christ's is a popular medium-sized college with nearly 400 under-graduates and 100 postgraduates.

ST ANDREW THE GREAT CHURCH

This very centrally located church, almost opposite the gatehouse of Christ's College, is a Victorian replacement on the site of a much older church taken down in 1842. Remodelled in the mid-1990s, it is now used by the parish of Holy Sepulchre (the Round Church). The building contains a memorial tablet to the family of Captain James Cook, explorer of the South Seas.

HOLY TRINITY CHURCH

Another centrally placed church, at the junction of Market and Sidney Streets, is basically medieval, with parts dating back to the twelfth century and numerous subsequent extensions and embellishments. Holy Trinity's slender spire, rebuilt in place of an earlier one in 1901, has long dominated this corner of town. From 1782 to 1836 this was the base of hymn-writer and preacher Charles Simeon (in 1799 one of the founders of the Church Missionary Society), who stamped upon it an Evangelical character which it retains.

44 *Holy Trinity Church in the early nineteenth century, with a view down Market Street. Print from R. Ackermann's* A History of the University of Cambridge *(1815).*

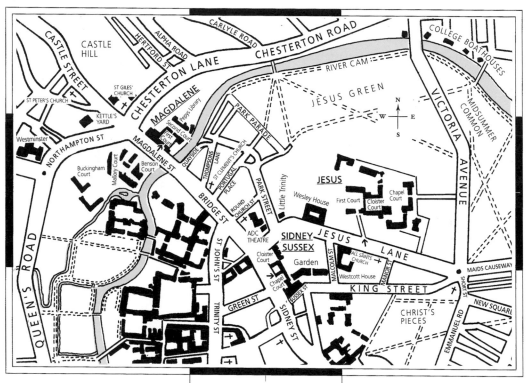

¼ MILE / 400 METRES

Arrows → indicate the usual tourist entrance to each college.

SIDNEY SUSSEX COLLEGE

Looming behind its wall fronting Sidney Street towards the junction with Jesus Lane, this college is known for its attractive gardens and for the head of Oliver Cromwell which is buried here. A nineteenth-century gothic archway leads past the porter's lodge and opens into two courts, left and right. Like Emmanuel, Sidney Sussex College (often known simply as Sidney) was built on the site of a friary abandoned after Henry VIII's Dissolution of the Monasteries: here friars of the Franciscan order had their lodgings. Although there are no visible remains of the friary, the lawned Cloister Court (through a passage to the north of Hall Court) now stands where the Franciscans' church once was. This verdant court is flanked to the east by an imposing red-brick and stone range (1891) in the neo-Jacobean style with Dutch gables and ornate bay windows. The present college chapel (1600, but rebuilt in 1782 and again from 1912 to 1923) is in the court to the right of the lodge. Its 'Edwardian' interior features attractive brown oak stalls and panels, coloured marble floor, bronze and marble altar, and decorative barrel-vaulting.

Sidney was founded in 1596 by an endowment left in the will of Lady Frances Sidney, Countess of Sussex (aunt of the Elizabethan poet Philip Sidney) in 1588. Its early buildings facing the street were converted in the 1820s and 30s by Sir Jeffrey Wyatville, whose controversial gables and stone facing altered the character of the site and still dominate from most directions. The young Oliver Cromwell had entered Sidney in 1616 and studied here for a year as a fellow commoner of the college, returning to Cambridge in 1643 to establish a garrison of Parliamentarian soldiers during the English Civil War and imprisoning the Master of his old college on account of the man's Royalist sympathies! Sidney accepted in 1960 a wooden cabinet containing an embalmed head impaled on a spiked metal pole – the head of Cromwell himself, preserved after his posthumous decapitation in 1661 and finally buried here 300 years later (commemorated by a plaque in the antechapel).

In the early nineteenth century Sidney gained a reputation for mathematics and science, and built its own chemistry and physics laboratory before the University itself had such facilities. Its beautifully kept garden, marking the extent of the

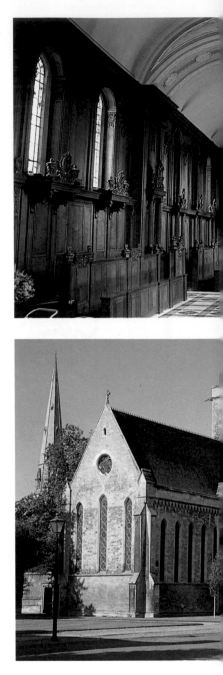

45 (top) *Interior of Sidney Sussex College Chapel.*

Franciscans' precinct, stretches to the north and east beyond the main courts and is visible from a covered passageway leading off next to the chapel.

Leaving via the porter's lodge, walking south down Sidney Street, and turning left into Sussex Street, we see ahead the college's own modern Bridge of Sighs – a simple but attractive structure of 1991 linking at the upper level two buildings belonging to the college.

JESUS COLLEGE

A few minutes' walk to the north east, off the beaten track for many tourists, the ancient courts of Jesus College are well worth a visit. The first college to take over the site of an old medieval priory, the nunnery of St Radegund, Jesus extended collegiate Cambridge into the fields on the edge of the old city, where it retains, with grounds leading towards the outreaches of the River Cam, a rural air. Dedicated in 1496 to 'the Blessed Virgin Mary, St John the Evangelist, and the Glorious Virgin St Radegund', but soon adopting its other name, associated with Jesus Lane and Jesus parish in which it was situated, Jesus College was the first of many Tudor foundations in Cambridge and Oxford; and one of its first students was a 14-year-old called Thomas Cranmer, later to be the great Tudor divine and author of the Book of Common Prayer.

Entered from Jesus Lane via a walled path known as The Chimney and an arch under the castellated red-brick gate-tower of about 1500 featuring a statue of the founder Bishop Alcock beneath his symbol (a cock perched on a globe), the college is built around the plan of the original nunnery buildings. Its highlights are the small Cloister Court, with an atmosphere closer than any other space in Cambridge to that of a medieval religious foundation (though this effect is mediated through several restorations); and the chapel, a smaller version of the original nuns' church, superbly restored and embellished by Victorian craftsmen. The original twelfth- and thirteenth-century fabric of the chapel is the oldest building to be incorporated within a Cambridge college.

First Court, reached immediately after the gate-tower and porter's lodge, is a good example of the hybrid but harmonious quality of many college sites in Cambridge. Based on monastic foundations but rebuilt and enlarged in the sixteenth, seventeenth, and nineteenth centuries, its architects over the years have remained sensitive to the aesthetic potential of the site, keeping the west side open (with the exception of a low wall) and preserving a unity among the buildings. The bronze horse on the lawn is by modern sculptor Barry Flanagan.

Access to Cloister Court is through a passage to the east. On the far side of this intimate cloister lie the remains, slightly sunken, of the arched doorway into the nuns' Chapter House, with a window on either side sporting stiff-leaf carving of about 1230. A passage just to the right leads to the massive, open-ended Chapel Court.

The darkness of the chapel interior, entered from Cloister Court, is relieved by coloured light filtered through windows in the nave and transepts (1873–7) by the Pre-Raphaelite artists William Morris, Edward Burne-Jones, and Ford Madox Brown, and in the chancel (1849–58) by Augustus Pugin. Galleries of Norman arches in the north transept (1150–75) provide indications of the original structure, while the chancel's narrow pointed lancet windows in the early-English gothic style belong to a thirteenth-century scheme much revised by Pugin (famous for his work on the Houses of Parliament), who also rebuilt the choir stalls. The attractive roof-painting in the crossing and nave is by William Morris.

It is worth ascending from the north-west corner of the cloister to the college hall, originally the refectory of the nunnery, with its roof (c.1500) of Spanish chestnut.

Apart from Cranmer, other famous Jesus

47 *'Hope, Faith, Charity': Pre-Raphaelite stained glass in Jesus College Chapel.*

students have included the writers Laurence Sterne, S. T. Coleridge, Alistair Cooke, and Jacob Bronowski; and Prince Edward, who read history here from 1983 to 1986.

Jesus owns a very fine Georgian town house known as Little Trinity (c.1725), set back at the end of a small walled garden where Jesus Lane meets Park Street and accommodating postgraduate students (see picture on p. 86).

ALL SAINTS CHURCH

The impressively spired church opposite Jesus is All Saints, built by G. F. Bodley in 1864. Like Jesus College Chapel, it contains stained glass (1865–6) by Pre-Raphaelites Morris, Burne-Jones, and Madox Brown. Constructed to replace the old All Saints on St John's Street (near where the Selwyn Divinity School now stands), the building remains consecrated but is maintained by the Redundant Churches Fund. It has been noted as an important landmark in the use of gothic forms by nineteenth-century English architects.

WESTCOTT HOUSE

Next to All Saints lies Westcott House, one of the four independent theological colleges in Cambridge. Here Anglican priests are trained. The college was founded in 1881; its street-facing range, part of a grassy inner court, dates from 1899.

WESLEY HOUSE

Further west, on the opposite side of Jesus Lane, the Methodist theological college Wesley House was established on its present site in 1925, having been founded in 1921. The newer buildings facing the road date from 1972.

ADC THEATRE

Across the street from the Jesus College house Little Trinity stands the theatre of the University's Amateur Dramatic Club, founded in 1855 and keenly supported by the Prince of Wales (later Edward VII), who arrived at Cambridge as an undergraduate in 1861. The present theatre building was opened in 1935.

ST CLEMENT'S CHURCH

Back on Bridge Street, on the way to Magdalene College, we pass the Church of St Clement, who became the patron saint of Danish sailors. This is the part of Cambridge developed by Danish invaders (yet to be Christianised) from c.875 AD: their port lay where Magdalene Bridge crosses the Cam. The present church building dates from after 1218, with many later additions including the street-facing tower of 1821. It now doubles as a Greek Orthodox church dedicated to St Athanasios.

MAGDALENE COLLEGE

Magdalene was a re-foundation, in 1542, of an older institution in the same buildings: a monastic hostel devoted to the education of scholar-monks. No other Cambridge college has this origin. Buckingham College, as it was known from about 1472, had been endowed on this site by four Benedictine abbeys (whose arms appear over some of the old doorways) and by the family of the dukes of Buckingham, but was dissolved by Henry VIII and re-opened as a secular college of the University with a dedication to St Mary Magdalene (pronounced 'maudlyn', and no doubt striking a chord with the name of its benefactor, Lord Audley, in keeping with the Renaissance love of punning). Original medieval brickwork (1470s) is visible in the range overlooking the river at Magdalene Bridge.

Until the early nineteenth century Magdalene remained the only part of the University on the far side of the river. Always a small college, its annual intake sometimes dwindling into single figures, it did not begin to expand until the early twentieth century under the Mastership of the man who wrote the words of *Land of Hope and Glory*, A. C. Benson. In the modern period Magdalene has attracted many notable figures, including Rudyard Kipling, Thomas Hardy, and T. S. Eliot (who were honorary fellows), I. A. Richards, C. S. Lewis, and Michael Ramsey (Archbishop of Canterbury, 1961–74).

Magdalene's entrance lies tight against the

street, diagonally opposite the sixteenth-century Pickerel Inn; and in past times this popular corner of town, just inside the entrance to the city at the foot of Castle Hill where the main routes from the north, east, and south converge, contained five inns in a row between the porter's lodge and the junction. Through the gate, First Court features a small chapel with a medieval oak roof, and to the left of it on the first floor rooms occupied from 1954 to 1963 by the celebrated Christian apologist C. S. Lewis, who was Professor of Medieval and Renaissance English in the University. On the first floor on 'C' staircase lived the Victorian poet and novelist Charles

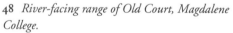

48 *River-facing range of Old Court, Magdalene College.*

49 (opposite) *Pepys Library, Magdalene College.*

Kingsley (author of *The Water-Babies*, 1863). To the east of the court stands the hall, where members of Magdalene preserve the ancient tradition of dining each night by candlelight, there being no electricity in the hall. Along with the Old Courts at Corpus Christi and Queens', Magdalene's First Court is the best encapsulation in Cambridge of the original medieval setting of domestic life in a college.

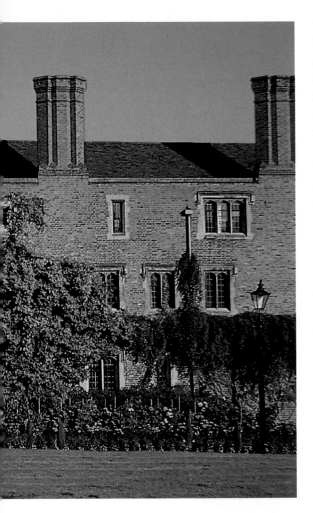

The architectural highlight of Magdalene, the late seventeenth-century Pepys Library Building with its attractive colonnaded stone façade in light Ketton stone, is found on the far side of Second Court. The diarist and secretary of the Admiralty Samuel Pepys died in 1703 and left to his college 3,000 volumes (including medieval manuscripts, early printed books by Caxton, Sir Francis Drake's nautical almanack, and his own famous diary), all arranged in the library in order of height. At the south end of the Pepys Building are rooms occupied in the mid-nineteenth century by the Irish nationalist politician C. S. Parnell, on the ground floor because of his tendency to sleepwalk.

Although still among the smallest colleges, Magdalene has expanded considerably in recent years, and a site on the other side of the street features Benson, Buckingham, and Mallory Courts – the last named after George Mallory, the Magdalene mountaineer who died in his unsuccessful attempt on Everest of 1924. The long west range of Benson Court was designed in brick by Edwin Lutyens, best known as the planner of New Delhi in India.

Closer to the street, early half-timbered buildings have been sensitively incorporated.

ST GILES'S CHURCH

At the south-east corner of Castle Street the large Anglican Church of St Giles dates mainly from 1875, but incorporates old aisle arches bearing witness to the former building on its site which existed from c.1092.

KETTLE'S YARD

Kettle's Yard, a combination of a house and gallery not far above the traffic lights on the other side of Castle Street, contains a first-rate collection of twentieth-century art, including works by Henri Gaudier-Brzeska, Ben Nicholson, Barbara Hepworth, and Henry Moore. The site was developed by art lover Jim Ede from four old cottages, accommodating a collection which he gave to the University of

Cambridge (still partly responsible for its maintenance) in 1966. The buildings, extended in the 1970s and again in the mid-1990s, provide an environment which has itself been described as a work of art.

ST PETER'S CHURCH

A little further up the hill, tucked away on a grassy bank behind trees, the very small Church of St Peter displays signs of its medieval origins, including a blocked doorway to the north and (inside) a carved font, both remnants of the Norman period. This is a peaceful spot, hidden from the bustling city just beneath it. More energetic visitors might continue up Castle Street to the site of Cambridge Castle itself, beyond the car park of the County Council buildings. All that remains of the castle is a rough motte (1068) commanding a view of the towers and spires it pre-dates.

50 *Tower and spire of St Peter's Church.*

The short entries in this final section relate to sites which lie away from central Cambridge, including all of the remaining University colleges and selected other places of interest connected with the University. They are presented in a roughly clockwise order starting with Newnham College to the south west of the city centre. All are marked on the general map of Cambridge at the beginning of this book. The first seven entries in particular (from Newnham to the University Library) comprise a walkable itinerary for the visitor with a bit more time but without motor transport.

51 (left) *Selwyn College gatehouse.*

52 (right) *Girton College gatehouse.*

53 *Schlumberger Building*

NEWNHAM COLLEGE

One of the most important and influential Oxbridge college foundations since the sixteenth century, Newnham (1871) set in motion a slow but distinct wave of feminist reform and was soon also setting new academic standards within the University. It has produced many leading women writers, scientists, and intellectuals and remains stalwartly an all-women college. Old Newnhamites include Sylvia Plath, Margaret Drabble, A. S. Byatt, Rosalind Franklin (whose work complemented that of Crick and Watson on the discovery of the structure of DNA), Germaine Greer (who still teaches here), and recent Oscar-winning actress Emma Thompson.

Newnham's early mentors were Henry Sidgwick, the moral philosopher and Cambridge professor who promoted women's education, and Anne Jemima Clough, its first Principal. The liberal aristocracy took an interest in the foundation, and the earliest students included Prime Minister's daughter Helen Gladstone, and Eleanor Balfour, sister of the future Prime Minister and later Mrs Sidgwick. In 1875 – by which time another women's college, Girton, had already been located in Cambridge – Clough took her growing assembly of students to the present site to the west of the male University. Here a parade of buildings in the Queen Anne style was being constructed by Basil Champneys, with Dutch red-brick gables and white woodwork, well suited to its setting around extensive lawns and flower beds. This is a highly attractive example of the Victorian taste for adapting older architectural styles on a grander scale in new environments, and a women's college presented Champneys with a challenge which he met with success. The scheme did not include a chapel (and the college still does without one).

By 1914 Newnham had more than 200 students, and during the First World War (with men called to serve abroad) it was larger than any of the male colleges. A significant step towards the acknowledgement that a University without women was a University cut off from a high proportion of the nation's intellect came in 1917 when Newnham received a college charter; and another was made in 1948 when women finally received University degrees.

RIDLEY HALL

Just east of Newnham stands Ridley Hall, conceived in 1877 as the first (with Wycliffe Hall, Oxford) of the Oxbridge theological colleges, and opening in 1881. Housed in buildings contemporary with those of Newnham next door, and with an allegiance to the Evangelical churches, the college remains largely independent of the University.

SIDGWICK SITE

On Sidgwick Avenue opposite Newnham College lies the principal site of the University's non-scientific faculties, named after moral philosopher Henry Sidgwick. Developed mainly in the 1960s, it provides lecture rooms and libraries for students of Classics, Economics, English, History, Law, Modern and Medieval Languages, Oriental Studies, and Philosophy, among others. Close to the road, the Museum of Classical Archaeology contains plaster casts of famous Greek and Roman sculptures including the Parthenon Frieze and the Delphi Charioteer. The importance of maintaining these replicas was emphasised when a terrorist bomb damaged one of the originals in Florence's Uffizi Gallery in 1993.

54 (top) *Newnham College: looking towards Clough Hall and the dining hall from the gardens.*

55 (bottom) *History Faculty Building, Sidgwick Site.*

On the far side of the site, the History Faculty Building (1964–8) by James Stirling has been one of Cambridge's most controversial, its bricks and bold glass front representing a kind of modernist experimentation both loved and despised; and next to it Norman Foster's arresting Squire Law Library, opened by the Queen in 1996.

SELWYN COLLEGE

George Augustus Selwyn, first Anglican Bishop of New Zealand, died in 1878 and was commemorated by the foundation of a new college closely associated with the Church of England. Opening in 1882 on Grange Road, Selwyn College (like its earlier counterpart in Oxford, Keble College) insisted that its senior members be confirmed Anglicans and maintain Christian principles. The Bishop had been a model of Victorian 'muscular Christianity', who as a St John's undergraduate in 1829 had rowed in the first Cambridge crew to race against Oxford and whose 'pure and heroic' English virtues were praised by Charles Kingsley in his dedication to *Westward Ho!* The Greek inscription above the college gateway means 'Stand fast in the faith and acquit yourselves like men.'

Selwyn became a favourite college for the sons of clergymen, different from the other Victorian Cambridge establishments (Girton, Newnham, Fitzwilliam, Homerton, Hughes Hall) which were inspired more by secular and social than ecclesiastical ideals. Its subsequent history has been one of gradual integration into the University. By 1926 it had achieved many of the privileges of the older colleges and in 1958 it was admitted as a full college of the University.

Selwyn's architecture is in the red-brick, neo-Tudor style of the 1880s, with a sturdy, turreted gate-tower in the front range set back from the street and a chapel reminiscent in shape (though not in scale) of the one built at King's College 400 years earlier.

CLARE HALL

Clare College contributed its name, money, and land to this postgraduate foundation of 1966, located to the west of the city beyond Grange Road. Major sponsorship also came from American foundations and Clare Hall specialises in places for senior scholars from overseas, offering more visiting fellowships than any other Cambridge college. Family-sized flats form part of an integrated architectural plan in a Scandinavian style, by Sweden-based architect Ralph Erskine. This small, friendly establishment, where students and scholars (and their spouses) share the common facilities, gained its full independence from Clare College in 1983.

ROBINSON COLLEGE

On Grange Road west of the University Library, Robinson (1977) is the newest of the Cambridge colleges, and the first foundation since Downing to have been set up with a massive donation from a single benefactor. A reclusive businessman who first made money selling bicycles in Bedford, David Robinson gave a total of £17m to finance a scheme which is, amongst other things, a distinct architectural success. Two tall ranges in Dorset multi-coloured brick form an inverted 'L' flanking the eastern and south-eastern ends of a large garden with woods and a brook, overlooked by rows of balconies. Between the tiered elevations runs the main college walkway, from which access is gained to a striking chapel with stained glass by well-known English artist John Piper.

On the day of opening by the Queen in 1981, Sir David Robinson supplemented his original donations with a further gift, but, increasingly immobile in his old age, was unable to attend

56 *Robinson College: west-facing range.*

57 *Tower of Cambridge University Library, by Giles Gilbert Scott.*

the ceremony. He died in 1987. A noted philanthropist, Robinson also funded (and named after his mother) the Rosie Maternity Hospital on Cambridge's Addenbrooke's site on Hills Road.

UNIVERSITY LIBRARY

Collections of books for common access have existed in the University since the 1300s, and in 1438 the first library room opened in the Old Schools, a site the University Library would occupy for nearly 500 years until it out-grew even the Cockerell Building there and moved, in 1934, into a massive purpose-built structure between Queen's Road and Grange Road. The architect of the new library was Giles Gilbert Scott, who designed Britain's old red telephone boxes to which the shape of the library tower has been likened. This is one of Britain's five Copyright Libraries, meaning that it must be offered a free copy of everything published in the UK. Although it does not accept every offer, Cambridge University Library nonetheless contains one of the fullest collections of books and manuscripts in the world, and is the largest open access library in Europe. Much of it computer-catalogued in the mid-1980s, its immense holdings are consulted by thousands of international scholars each year. Admission for those not members of the University is by special ticket only.

ISAAC NEWTON INSTITUTE

On Clarkson Road (off the northern end of Grange Road), the University's Institute for Mathematical Sciences is an advanced study centre where mathematicians and scientists from around the world can pursue research projects. It was opened in 1992 and named after Cambridge's greatest scientific thinker, born 350 years earlier.

WESTMINSTER COLLEGE

Back nearer the city centre, Westminster is the United Reformed Church's theological college, set up in Cambridge in 1899 as a Presbyterian centre, on the corner where Madingley Road meets Northampton Street. Its warm brick and stone make an attractive façade, rising above a stony concourse behind high railings where the road bends. A former Cambridge theological college, Cheshunt, joined with Westminster on this site in 1967.

58 *Møller Centre for Continuing Education, Churchill College.*

LUCY CAVENDISH COLLEGE

In a garden setting just to the west, Britain's first University college for mature women (aged 21 and over) is accommodated in a blend of Victorian and modern buildings. Lucy Cavendish College is authorised to employ only women academics, to help redress the balance of women to men in higher education. Opened in 1965, this is the smallest of the University of Cambridge's 31 colleges, containing about 150 students (two thirds at undergraduate level). Lucy Cavendish (1841–1925), daughter-in-law of the founder of the Cavendish Laboratory, was an advocate of women's education.

ST EDMUND'S COLLEGE

On nearby Mount Pleasant stand buildings opened for the accommodation of Roman Catholic students in 1896 and converted into a postgraduate college in 1965. The name (until 1986 St Edmund's House) commemorates not the well-known patron saint of East Anglia but a thirteenth-century Archbishop of Canterbury called Edmund. With a complement of nearly 200 students (who need not nowadays be Catholic), this remains the only college in the University with a Roman Catholic chapel. Modern extensions culminate in the street-facing tower (1992), a structure which draws on different architectural idioms and is topped by the highest room in any Cambridge college.

CHURCHILL COLLEGE

Winston Churchill did not go to university, but when he retired as Prime Minister in 1955 one of his ambitions was to set up a college of advanced technology. In 1958 Churchill College was launched, opening in 1960 half a mile up Madingley Road to the west, on a scale unsurpassed except by the larger of the older colleges. The college has, uniquely, a 70:30 ratio of science to arts students; an unusually high proportion of postgraduates; and a vigorous programme of overseas visiting fellowships. Always committed to modernity, Churchill boasts the first flats in Cambridge designed for married postgraduates, a garden sculpture by Barbara Hepworth, and the distinction of being the first undergraduate college to decide to become co-residential. Sir Winston's papers inaugurated an archive of political, scientific, and military records in the Archives Centre, to which the papers of former Labour party leader Neil Kinnock have lately been added.

In 1992 the Møller Centre for Continuing Education was opened here: the gift of a Danish benefactor, designed by a Danish architect.

OBSERVATORIES AND WEST CAMBRIDGE SITE

On gentle slopes above Madingley Road, beyond Churchill, the grand early nineteenth-century neo-classical architecture of the observatories still forms the centre of astronomical science in Cambridge. The Northumberland 12-inch refracting telescope is in the largest of the domes. This was briefly the world's biggest telescope: in 1846 James Challis used it in a (fruitless) search for the planet Neptune. Strong traditions of theoretical and radio astronomy in the University (for which Antony Hewish and Martin Ryle won the Nobel Prize for Physics in 1974) attracted the Royal Greenwich Observatory here in 1990, when it moved from the site in Herstmonceux, Sussex, that it had occupied since relocating in 1950 from Greenwich itself (where it was founded in 1675). This Madingley Rise complex also houses a satellite tracking station used for studies of continental drift. The University's Mullard Radio Astronomy Observatory may also be seen, from the A603 beyond Barton four miles south west of Cambridge, its array of radio telescopes following the course of the old railway line to Oxford, which provided a site that was conveniently straight and flat. Neutron stars were discovered here in 1967.

On the south side of Madingley Road the West Cambridge Site houses the new Cavendish Laboratory (where the University's Department of Physics is based) as well as the Faculty of Clinical Veterinary Medicine (one of the United Kingdom's six veterinary schools) and the Whittle Engineering Laboratory. Further along the road on the same side may be seen important centres attracted to Cambridge partly because of the University: the dramatically modern building of Schlumberger Cambridge Research; and the headquarters of the British Antarctic Survey.

AMERICAN CEMETERY

Though on former University land, the American Cemetery (near Madingley, three miles west of Cambridge) is not part of the University. A memorial to countless American servicemen who died in Europe during the Second World War, many of them from air force bases scattered across East Anglia, its chapel and hillside site attract many transatlantic visitors.

MADINGLEY HALL

The University's Board of Continuing Education has its headquarters in a Tudor mansion in rolling countryside above Madingley village. Here well-attended residential courses are organised throughout the year, all open for enrolment to members of the public. The gateway (*c.*1470) leading to the old stables yard is that which stood at the front of the east front of the Old Schools until Stephen Wright's reconstruction of the 1750s.

GIRTON COLLEGE

No women's college existed in Cambridge or Oxford when in 1869 educational reformer Emily Davies set up a female establishment, on the Cambridge collegiate model, in Hitchin, Hertfordshire, to prepare students for the Cambridge tripos. The spirit of reform was strong, and by the time she moved in 1873 to a spacious site on the edge of Girton village, two and a half miles north west of the city, another women's college (the forerunner of Newnham) had already been founded in Cambridge. Change occurred slowly and Girton received its formal college charter in 1924. Until the second half of the twentieth century it and Newnham remained the only two female colleges in a University that continued to be dominated by men.

Girton is a showpiece of 1870s red-brick architecture by the prolific Alfred Waterhouse. Its tower, turrets, and gables are visible against the lush fields on the north-western approach to the city. Following the co-educational reforms of the 1960s and 70s Girton admitted men, who now account for over half of its student numbers, making this the third largest of the colleges at first-degree level, with over 500 undergraduates (as well as 100 or more postgraduates). Uniquely among Cambridge colleges, the fellowship of Girton is evenly balanced between women and men.

59 *The unique architecture of the dining hall, Fitzwilliam College.*

FITZWILLIAM COLLEGE

The origins of this modern college go back to the formation of the Non-Collegiate Students Board in 1869. The Board's headquarters were established at 31 and 32 Trumpington Street, near the Fitzwilliam Museum, and became known in 1887 as Fitzwilliam Hall and in 1924 as Fitzwilliam House. When full collegiate status was gained in 1966, the college moved to its present site on Huntingdon Road, on the way out towards Girton.

The highlights of Fitzwilliam's modernist architecture are the dining hall by Denys Lasdun, with its unusual lantern of hooded arches and high, clear glass windows; and the internationally acclaimed chapel by Richard MacCormac, who also built New Court. A Victorian house, The Grove, has been sympathetically incorporated into the college's eight-acre grounds.

NEW HALL

Near the city side of Fitzwilliam lies New Hall, founded in 1954 to provide more places for women in the University. The college now has about 300 undergraduates and 80 postgraduates, with a mixed fellowship of men and women. Its buildings, erected here in 1962–4 on land originally occupied and then donated by descendants of Charles Darwin, have recently received a Grade II architectural listing. Of special note are the elegantly articulated dome of the dining hall, and the fine library with its vaulted roof, both forming the centre of Fountain Court. A new entrance court and a further residential block that will help house all of the college's students on the same site are to be built following a generous benefaction. Recent donations of over 100 paintings and sculptures by leading women artists have created a collection unique in Britain, and this is open for display. New Hall provided the first woman Vice-Chancellor of the University, Rosemary Murray (who was also the college's first President), as well as the University's first woman Treasurer, Joanna Womack.

60 *College rowers training on the Cam.*

JESUS GREEN AND RIVER CAM

Along Chesterton Lane a footbridge leads to Jesus Green, a public recreational area which is an ideal starting-point for river walks. Here a Protestant martyr, John Hullier of King's College, was burned at the stake for his faith in the mid-sixteenth century; and here in the nineteenth century plans were made (but never fulfilled) to build a railway station. A weir lies on the Cam, and further east there is an outdoor swimming pool.

Visitors with more time should strike out along the river path, under the Victoria Road bridge, and on across Midsummer Common and Stourbridge Common, where an annual fair took place for more than 500 years from the early 1200s, attracting traders and theatrical entertainers from all over Europe in Elizabethan times and becoming the largest gathering of its kind in Europe. On the north bank the college boathouses are feverish with activity early in the mornings during term, as rowers limber up and gather their oars. At most times of the year it is possible to see boat crews in training on this stretch of river and, indeed, all the way down to Chesterton and Baits Bite Lock a few miles away, where the annual 'Lents' and 'May Bumps' (intercollegiate rowing competitions) take place. Rowing is the best known of many sports pursued at a high level by Cambridge University students, some of whom will win a Blue by competing in their chosen sport against Oxford. A select few rowers make it into the Boat Race, the annual contest with Oxford on the River Thames in London, which continues to compel worldwide interest.

SCIENCE PARK

In the 1980s the University and colleges helped fund Cambridge's expansion as an international centre of technological development, and the Science Park, founded by Trinity College as the first of its kind in the country, is a thriving testimony to this impetus. It lies two and a half miles north of the city where the A1309/A10 Ely road reaches the A45 bypass: the monumental NAPP Laboratories (1981–3), with their huge white frames and glass fronts, are imposingly visible from the road. Computer and pharmaceutical companies are among the businesses which make this high-tech industrial estate, retaining close research links with the University, a success.

graduate) are on display. The statue in the garden was cast by Scott's widow Kathleen.

Alongside, the University's Department of Chemistry (built 1953–60) is a major centre for Organic and Inorganic Chemistry inspired by Lord Todd, winner of the Nobel Prize in 1957; and nearby, Tennis Court Road heads north towards the Downing Site. Along this street we find, on the west side, the Department of Pharmacology, Institute of Biotechnology, and Wellcome Trust and Cancer Research Campaign Institute of Cancer and Developmental Biology; and further along to the east, the Department of Biochemistry, which has, with the Medical Research Council's Cambridge laboratories, been responsible for leading research projects in the biochemical field, impelled by the work done in Cambridge on proteins and nucleic acids by Fred Sanger, the first person to win two Nobel Prizes for Chemistry (in 1958 and 1980).

HUGHES HALL

Located a mile to the east of the city centre overlooking Fenner's, the University cricket ground, Hughes Hall began in 1885 as the Cambridge Training College for Women Teachers. It moved in 1895 into new red-brick buildings reminiscent of those at Newnham (the college which helped set it up) and in 1949 changed its name in commemoration of Miss E. P. Hughes, its first Principal. Men were first admitted in 1973 to read for higher degrees and diplomas, when Hughes Hall became a graduate college of the University.

SCOTT POLAR RESEARCH INSTITUTE AND TENNIS COURT ROAD AREA

On Lensfield Road, west of the Catholic Church, an institute named after Captain Robert Falcon Scott, the British explorer who died having reached the South Pole in 1912, is devoted to research relating to the polar regions. Opened in 1920, the institute includes a public museum featuring exhibits of Arctic and Antarctic exploration. Letters discovered with the bodies of the ill-fated explorers of 1912 (including Dr Edward Wilson, a Cambridge

HOMERTON COLLEGE

Homerton is the University's College of Education where school teachers are trained. Here they study for their Bachelor of Education degree, awarded by the University. Homerton achieved collegiate status within the University in 1976; but its history began well before that, in 1768, when Homerton Academy (at Homerton in east London) was established to educate ministers for the nonconformist Congregationalist church. The emphasis shifted to teacher-training by the time the institution moved to Cambridge in 1894, taking over the red-brick complex built in the 1870s for the ill-starred Cavendish College (which was opened in 1876 but closed in 1892) on Hills Road, a mile and a half south of the city. Now mixed, Homerton was a women's college between 1895 and 1978.

BOTANIC GARDEN

About a mile south of the city centre, between Trumpington Road and Hills Road, lies the University Botanic Garden, which occupies approximately 40 acres of pleasantly landscaped grounds with many mature specimen trees, some found very rarely in cultivation. It was opened in 1846 to supersede a much smaller garden set up in 1762 where the New Museums Site now is. The modern garden contains a glasshouse range with a recently rebuilt tropical unit, an attractive limestone rock garden by the lake, and specialised collections of hardy plants including a unique 'chronological bed' in which familiar plants are displayed in order of their date of introduction into British gardens. On the eastern side there is a special scented garden planted with aromatic species for the blind.

WOLFSON COLLEGE

While the other foundations of the 1960s were spawned with support from existing colleges or non-University sources, the new college on Barton Road, to the south west beyond Newnham, was established by the University itself in 1965. Financial independence was achieved by the fledgling 'University College' on 1 January 1973 when the Wolfson Foundation (created by Scottish philanthropist Isaac Wolfson) provided it with £2m and a new name. Its modern buildings form an 'E' shape on a thoughtfully laid-out site. Though begun as a postgraduate institution, Wolfson now gives about 20 per cent of its places to undergraduates, but maintains a minimum entry age of 21.

61 *The University Botanic Garden.*

GLOSSARY

There follows a list, with brief explanations, of University-related terms used in this guidebook. Geoffrey Skelsey's *About Cambridge: the Way it Works: an Unofficial Guide to the Organisation and Procedures of the University of Cambridge* (available from the University Registry) is gratefully acknowledged as a source for some of this information.

BA

The BA, or Bachelor of Arts, is the name of the primary degree obtained by most Cambridge University students after successfully completing their undergraduate course of study and tripos examinations in the University. Undergraduates at Homerton College sit for a BEd (Bachelor of Education) degree. Cambridge students reading medicine or veterinary medicine take a BA in an appropriate subject and then pursue an extended course of study leading to e.g. the MB (Bachelor of Medicine), BChir (Bachelor of Surgery), or VetMB (Bachelor of Veterinary Medicine); and there are also Bachelors' degrees in Divinity and Music. See also MA and Doctorate below.

BACKS

The Backs is the name given to the kilometre stretch of riverbank and adjoining college grounds running from Darwin College in the south to Magdalene College in the north.

BLUE

Anyone competing for Cambridge against the University of Oxford in one of a range of particular sports wins a Blue, which includes the entitlement to wear a special blazer in the Cambridge sky-blue colour. Some sports merit a Half-Blue rather than the full award, meaning that the blazer must be tempered with buff. Cambridge's distinctive colour is thought to

originate in the Boat Race against Oxford of 1836, when the Cambridge boat, lacking proper colours at its bow, was decorated in a makeshift ribbon which happened to be sky-blue.

CHANCELLOR

The Duke of Edinburgh has, since 1977, filled the role of titular head of the University of Cambridge. As Chancellor, elected by the Senate, he has certain statutory duties, his principal public responsibility in modern times being the conferment of honorary degrees.

COLLEGE

Readers are referred to pp. 1–2 for a discussion of what a college is and how it functions within, and in relation to, the public University.

COURT

A Cambridge court is an inner yard, usually surrounded on three or more sides by buildings, found within the colleges, the Old Schools, etc. In Oxford (but never in Cambridge) courts are known as quadrangles.

ÐEAN

The Dean of a college is usually the fellow, generally an ordained priest, with responsibility for the college chapel and its services, although in some colleges the title is used of the official responsible for internal discipline.

DEPARTMENT

A department is a subdivision of a University faculty (see below), more common in science than in arts subjects. For example, the Departments of Genetics and Plant Sciences are part of the Faculty of Biology 'A', while the Faculty of Mathematics includes the Department of Applied Mathematics and Theoretical Physics, and the Department of Pure Mathematics and Mathematical Statistics. Non-scientific departments include those of French, German, and Italian, all part of the Faculty of Modern and Medieval Languages.

DIRECTOR OF STUDIES

A Director of Studies is appointed by a college to advise on and oversee the work of students in that college taking a particular subject.

DOCTORATE

A doctorate is the degree of doctor, most often in Cambridge a PhD (i.e. Doctorate of Philosophy). This is a senior degree, higher than the BA or MA, and is usually achieved after three years of postgraduate study. Higher doctorates, such as the LLD (Doctorate of Law) or DD (Doctorate of Divinity) are the most senior qualifications in the University, and are usually conferred on those who have published extensive original works in their field.

DON

This old-fashioned colloquial term, now falling out of use in Cambridge, derives from the Latin word 'dominus' (lord, master, sir) and denotes any senior member of the University or of a college, including professors, lecturers, and Directors of Studies.

FACULTY

Each of Cambridge's faculties is an administrative subdivision of the University responsible for teaching and research within a particular academic subject or group of subjects. Examples are the Faculties of Classics, Clinical Medicine, Education, Engineering, Music, and Oriental Studies. Some of the larger faculties are divided into departments (see above), for administrative convenience.

FELLOW

A fellow (who may in most colleges be male or female) is a senior member of a college. The fellowship of a college might include full, research, visiting, honorary, and emeritus fellows, and fellow commoners, all with differing degrees and types of status and responsibility. Fellows often (though not necessarily) have teaching and administrative duties within the college.

FRESHER

An undergraduate student in his or her first year is known as a fresher.

GOWNS AND HOODS

Undergraduates of each college have a distinctive knee-length gown, usually black (exceptions being the gowns of Trinity and Caius, which are dark blue). These are worn on formal occasions including visits to the Senate-House, to dinner (in the case of some of the colleges), and (occasionally) to teaching sessions with the Director of Studies. A hood is worn with the gown at the graduation ceremony. MA and doctorate degrees entitle the holder to a different status of gown.

GRADUATION

This ceremony takes place in the Senate-House about ten times a year. Graduands from each college parade together in formal dress to receive their degrees. Special ceremonies each June, known as General Admission, are the occasions when the majority of students receive their BA degrees after three years of study.

HIGH TABLE

Most of the colleges preserve a formal dining arrangement, with fellows and their guests sitting together at a special table, separate from the student body. In the older halls the High Table stands at one end, at right angles to the student tables, and may be raised above them on a dais.

HONORARY DEGREE

This is a special degree, usually at the doctorate level, awarded to a person of great distinction, either from the UK or elsewhere. It is often conferred by the Chancellor himself, at a colourful ceremony held each June.

MA

The MA (Cantab) is the Master of Arts degree, for which Cambridge graduates become eligible six years after the end of their first term of residence in the University.

MASTER

The Master of a college is its head, usually elected by the other fellows for a limited term, and in some cases appointed from outside. All of the colleges in the University have Masters except for Clare Hall, Hughes Hall, Lucy Cavendish, New Hall, Queens', and Wolfson, which call their heads Presidents instead; Homerton and Newnham, which have Principals; Girton, a Mistress; King's, a Provost; and Robinson, a Warden. All of these may be known colloquially as 'Heads of Houses'.

MATRICULATION

Although a University matriculation ceremony has not taken place since 1962, all new Cambridge students must still enrol or register with their college by signing a declaration that they will obey the regulations, thus formally matriculating. The word comes from the Latin 'matrix', meaning roll or register. 'Coming up' is a colloquial term often used in place of 'matriculating'.

OXBRIDGE

This contraction means Oxford and Cambridge – i.e. the two most ancient of the British universities – and usually also connotes the type of education, based on the college system, offered here.

PhD

See Doctorate, above.

PORTER

All of the colleges have porters, who are members of the college staff with a range of responsibilities normally directed by a Head Porter. To students and visitors alike, the porter is most familiar as the figure who occupies the porter's lodge at the college entrance, answering queries, guarding the gate, handing out keys, and harbouring a fund of information about domestic arrangements within the college.

POSTGRADUATE

A postgraduate is a student with a first degree from Cambridge or elsewhere, now studying for a higher degree.

PUNT

In Cambridge or Oxford, punters are people who propel or ride in the long, flat boats that can be seen on the river at virtually any time of the year and, during term, at most times of the day or night. There are public punt-hire stations at the Mill Pond (Granta Place), Quayside (Magdalene Bridge), and elsewhere. Chauffeurs may also be hired. Pleasure punting of this kind developed in the late nineteenth century, in boats based on fishing and cargo vessels used in earlier years to navigate the shallow waters of the Thames Valley. The trend reached Cambridge in about 1902 and is now, in spite of its widespread national popularity during the Edwardian years, almost exclusively an Oxbridge pursuit.

REGENT HOUSE

The Regent House is a body of about 3,000 members composed mainly of teaching and administrative officers from the University and colleges. Representatives of this body congregate from time to time in the Senate-House to vote upon matters relating to the legislation, constitution, and actions of the corporate University.

SENATE

Holders of Cambridge degrees at MA level or higher comprise the University Senate.

STATUTE

The University of Cambridge is governed by a framework of statutes drawn up in 1926 and based on a constitutional code dating from the thirteenth century. Amendments (of which there have been many since 1926) require the approval of The Queen in Council.

SYNDICATE

A committee set up to oversee a particular function or activity within the University, sometimes academic and sometimes administrative, is known as a syndicate. It includes senior members of the University drawn from various areas. Examples are the Library Syndicate, Lodgings Syndicate, Sports Syndicate, and University Press Syndicate.

TRIPOS

This is the name given to a Cambridge examination leading to a first degree, usually the Bachelor of Arts. The word derives from the Greco-Latin for a 'three-legged stool' and refers to the object on which the examiner used to sit while listening to candidates offering oral defences of their work before the introduction of written examinations. Unique to Cambridge, this sense of the word has been in use here since at least the sixteenth century.

UNDERGRADUATE

An undergraduate is a student studying for a first degree, normally the Bachelor of Arts. Most Cambridge undergraduates are in their late teens or early twenties, but there are also mature students who matriculate at a later age.

VICE-CHANCELLOR

The Vice-Chancellor, assisted by a Pro-Vice-Chancellor and a number of Deputy Vice-Chancellors, oversees the administration of the University and is its principal full-time resident officer, with a number of important ceremonial and statutory duties. He or she is appointed for a period of up to seven years.

For more detailed discussions of Cambridge's architecture, the reader is referred to *The Buildings of England: Cambridgeshire*, by Nikolaus Pevsner (Penguin Books, 1954; 2nd edition, 1970), *Cambridge Architecture*, by Tim Rawle (Trefoil Books, 1985; 2nd edition André Deutsch Limited, 1993), and the works by Nicholas Ray and Willis and Clark listed below. What follows is a selection of useful books on Cambridge published by Cambridge University Press, all available from the Press's bookshop at 1 Trinity Street.

The Architectural History of the University of Cambridge: Volumes I, II, and III, by Robert Willis and John Willis Clark, reissued 1988

Bedders, Bulldogs and Bedells: A Cambridge Glossary, by Frank Stubbings, 1995

Cambridge and Clare, by Harry Godwin, 1985

Cambridge Commemorated, compiled by Laurence and Helen Fowler, 1984

Cambridge in the Age of the Enlightenment: Science, Religion and Politics from the Restoration to the French Revolution, by John Gascoigne, 1989

Cambridge Minds, edited by Richard Mason, 1994

Cambridge University Library: A History: From the Beginnings to the Copyright Act of Queen Anne, by J. C. T. Oates, 1986

Cambridge University Library: A History: The Eighteenth and Nineteenth Centuries, by D. J. McKitterick, 1984

Cambridge Women: Twelve Portraits, edited by Edward Shils and Carmen Blacker, 1996

A Concise Guide to Cambridge Architecture, by Nicholas Ray, 1994

A Concise History of the University of Cambridge, by Elisabeth Leedham-Green, 1996

A History of Addenbrooke's Hospital, Cambridge, by Arthur Rook, Margaret Carlton, and W. Graham Cannon, 1992

A History of Cambridge University Press: Volume I: Printing and the Book Trade in Cambridge, 1534–1698, by D. J. McKitterick, 1992

A History of Cambridge University Press, 1584–1984, by M. H. Black, 1984

A History of the University of Cambridge: Volume I: The University to 1546, by Damien Riehl Leader, 1989

A History of the University of Cambridge: Volume IV: 1870–1990, by Christopher Brooke, 1992

Le Keux's Engravings of Victorian Cambridge, edited by L. P. Wilkinson (with a Foreword by the Duke of Edinburgh), 1985

A Literary History of Cambridge, by Graham Chainey, reissued 1994

Oxford and Cambridge, by Christopher Brooke and Roger Highfield (with photographs by Wim Swaan), 1988

An Oxford View of Cambridge: With Some Reflections on Oxford and Other Universities, by Lord Jenkins of Hillhead, 1988

A Short History of Cambridge University Press, by M. H. Black, 1992

University Politics: F. M. Cornford's Cambridge and his Advice to the Young Academic Politician, by Gordon Johnson, 1994

62 (above) *Restored half-timbered residence: Benson Court, Magdalene College.*

63 (below) *Georgian town house, now a Jesus College residence: Little Trinity, Jesus Lane.*

INDEX

Published by the Press Syndicate of the University of Cambridge
The Pitt Building, Trumpington Street, Cambridge CB2 IRP
40 West 20th Street, New York, NY 10011-4211, USA
10 Stamford Road, Oakleigh, Melbourne 3166, Australia

First published 1994
Reprinted 1996, 1997

Printed in Great Britain at the University Press, Cambridge

A catalogue record for this book is available from the British Library

Library of Congress cataloguing in publication data applied for

ISBN 0 521 45913 3 paperback

INSIDE BACK COVER *Elizabethan Cambridge: George Braun's plan of Cambridge dating from 1575 (top), and John Hammond's drawing of 1592. Many of today's familiar landmarks are already in place, and the main street system is more or less the same. Note on the Hammond drawing the different layout of the courts at Trinity and St John's Colleges, and the Greyfriars' precinct of the Franciscans, where Sidney Sussex College now lies.*